Paris
Secrets

CELTIC RUN: BOOK 1

While in Ireland on a class trip, Jake stumbles upon the first clue to a treasure missing from the Spanish Armada. Jake sees the riches as his chance to buy back the family sailboat and restore a piece of the life he enjoyed before his father was critically injured in an accident. Desperate to find the treasure, Jake teams up with Zach, his nemesis and class bully, and two girls in a clue-hunting chase across the Dingle Peninsula. Dodging would-be thieves, exchanging wisecracks with Zach, and concocting ingenious devices to get them out of scrapes, Jake leads the team as they connect piece after piece to the more than 400-year-old mystery.

CHICAGO BOUND: BOOK 2

Jake's plan for a carefree holiday at a musical performing arts camp in the Windy City hits a sour note when he stumbles upon a long-hidden message from his late mother, art historian Karen McGreevy. She had traveled to Chicago 13 years earlier on a dream assignment, never to return home. With his violin and his mother's mysterious letter in hand, Jake, his best friend Julie, and new pals Ben and Natalie are heading west, where they will follow the clues and uncover the truth about a missing masterpiece, the meaning of friendship, and the enduring bond between a mother and her son.

PARIS SECRETS: BOOK 3

HOW DO A BAKING CONTEST AND A MISSION FROM WORLD WAR II COMBINE? WITH A WHISK . . . AND SOME RISK!

This third book in the series finds Jake and his best friend, Ben Meyers, as partners in a televised baking contest at the famed Le Cordon Bleu cooking school in Paris during spring break. In their spare time, the two are determined to search for answers regarding a 1940 photograph that belonged to Jake's late mother. Who is this family? Are they related to Jake? And what does the cryptic note that is written on the back mean? As they discover clues and make new friends along the way, Jake and Ben find themselves on the journey of a lifetime.

A Jake McGreevy Novel

Paris Secrets

SEAN VOGEL

MB PUBLISHING

ISBN:
Softcover: 978-0-9850814-3-0

Library of Congress Control Number: 2021931804

Summary: While in Paris over spring break for a baking contest, Jake McGreevy and his best friend Ben Meyers also solve a mystery from the perilous days of World War II, making friends and finding family along the way.

Graphic design and cover: PageWave Graphics, Inc., www.pagewavegraphics.com

Photo Credits
COVER:
Eiffel Tower on the Seine River ©istockphoto.com/Apilart; Colorful macarons ©istockphoto.com/jirkaejc; Textured, blue-painted canvas ©istockphoto.com/enjoynz

CHAPTERS:
Prologue: Blue ribbon ©istockphoto.com/miss_J; 1: Lead pencil ©istockphoto.com/hayatikayhan; 2: Little red kitten ©istockphoto.com/Litvalifa; 3: Ornate brass knocker ©istockphoto.com/UroshPetrovic; 4: Rugelach cookies ©istockphoto.com/MentalArt; 5: Daffodils ©istockphoto.com/aluxum; 6: Stainless steel wire whisk ©istockphoto.com/Adam Smigielski; 7: Chevrolet Deluxe 1950 ©istockphoto.com/Anton_Sokolov; 8: Kick city rider bike ©istockphoto.com/Nature; 9: Blue sweater ©istockphoto.com/kokoroyuki; 10: World globe ©istockphoto.com/EMPPhotography; 11: Jar with raspberry jam and raspberries ©istockphoto.com/IngaNielsen; 12: Unwrapped chewing gums ©istockphoto.com/filistimlyanin; 13: Paper clip ©istockphoto.com/moonisblack; 14: Colorful shopping bags ©istockphoto.com/deliormanli; 15: Crêpes and chocolate ©istockphoto.com/margouillatphotos; 16: Stack of dark chocolate baking bar pieces ©istockphoto.com/viennetta; 17: Golden music notes and treble clef on musical strings ©istockphoto.com/Bet_Noire; 18: Green teacup and teabag ©istockphoto.com/karandaev; 19: Life buoy ©istockphoto.com/H20addict; 20: Bunny ©istockphoto.com/chengyuzheng; 21: Baklavas ©istockphoto.com/subjug; 22: Frog ©istockphoto.com/kerkla; 23: Mobile phone with key ©istockphoto.com/scanrail; 24: Violin ©istockphoto.com/J-Elgaard; 25: Red book ©istockphoto.com/robynmac; 26: Napoleon pastry ©istockphoto.com/Juanmonino; 27: Wooden match ©istockphoto.com/Poligrafistka; 28: Russian samovar ©istockphoto.com/fyb; 29: Flour in sack ©istockphoto.com/Alter_photo; 30: Chocolate cake slice ©istockphoto.com/unalozmen; 31: The French Légion d'honneur medal ©istockphoto.com/olemac; 32: Fortune cookie ©istockphoto.com/dlerick

This book is dedicated to the men, women, and children who stand up against hatred and injustice around the world. Only through their courageous acts can we hope to overcome evil and experience the full joy life has to offer.

And to Margie, for her help, friendship, and enduring patience in telling this story.

PROLOGUE

German-Occupied Paris
Tuesday, July 7, 1942
10:28 pm

An unseasonably cold wind whipped through the slender woman's wool overcoat, chilling her to the bone. *I can't be late—not tonight,* she thought, as she hurried down the street of the darkened city. The curfew had been in effect since 8:00 p.m. In her imagination, every one of her footsteps sounded alarmingly loud. In reality, though, she had mastered moving with the speed and stealth of a rabbit on high alert.

Ahead of her, the rumble from an approaching truck echoed off the granite walls of a nearby shop. Holding her breath, the woman flattened against the door. *Please don't see me,* she prayed. As the truck sped past, she curled her lip at the sight of the swastika painted on its side.

Rounding the corner, she arrived at a heavy glass and metal door, turned the handle, slipped quickly into the building, and then quietly entered the apartment at the end of the hall. There seemed to be little difference between the dim light cast by the waning crescent moon and the total blackness inside. When she fumbled to lock the door, a small light was switched on behind her.

"Oh, you startled me!" she said in a hushed voice. In actuality, it was the odor of lactic acid that surprised her. She never could grow accustomed to that chemical smell, but she knew she shouldn't complain about that lifesaving tool in every forger's tool kit.

"My apologies, but thank you for being on time," a young man replied. She saw that he wore dark pants, a crisp shirt, black suspenders, and a look of utter exhaustion.

"Of course."

"I believe these are our best yet." He gestured toward three sets of false papers laid out on a table: identity cards, passports, a marriage certificate, food ration cards, birth and baptismal certificates, and library cards.

The woman put on her glasses to inspect the work up close. "Yes, I agree," she said, after several minutes. "These *are* fine. Not one error." The paper, the stamps, the ink colors, the signatures—all would pass even the most meticulous scrutiny. "You really are an incredible artist. And for cards that are brand-new, they look perfectly aged. *Merci beaucoup.*" The woman hugged the man with whom she'd worked before but whose given name, for security reasons, was still unknown to her. She knew him only by his code name: Night Watch.

Separating the papers into three stacks, she tied each with a ribbon of a different color and slid each set inside a medium-size envelope. Then she tucked them into her satchel beneath a large bag of sandwiches, taking care not to crush the precious papers.

"May our God and the God of our ancestors lead us toward peace, guide our footsteps toward peace, and make us reach our desired destination for life, gladness, and peace," Night Watch whispered, as they stood by the door.

The woman nodded and looked straight into his fresh face, finishing the Traveler's Prayer: "And may our God rescue us from the hand of every foe and ambush." As she slowly turned the knob and opened the door a bit, the young man peered into the hall and then gave her his okay to hurry toward the main entrance of the building. In a moment, she was outside again in the wind, her silent steps now even quicker than before. Her chest tightened as she thought about what she was about to do—what she was being forced to do.

After a few blocks, she came to the door of a stationery shop and gave it a single rap with her knuckles. It swung open immediately, and as she swept past the man who had admitted her, she tapped his shoulder in greeting. Inside, a small lantern tried valiantly to light the back room where a woman sat waiting with a sullen-looking girl at her side. The girl brightened and leapt to her feet when she saw who had come in.

"Mama!" she whisper-yelled. The girl, age 11, was dressed in traveling clothes and holding a small knapsack. The woman bent down to greet her with a warm embrace.

To the male and female escort, she said, "Everything is ready. Here is your paperwork. Brave souls have risked everything to provide these. They are as good as authentic and should give you no trouble." She hugged her colleagues in the underground and then, once more, bent to draw her daughter, Esther, close.

"Mama, why can't you come with me?" she said, wrapping her arms tightly around her mother's neck. Her two younger sisters had already been whisked away, far from France, for safety. Papa was gone. Now this.

"Remember, *chérie?*" the woman said, crouching beside her daughter and taking her hand. "I made a pledge to our friends and neighbors of the 20th *arrondissement.* You mustn't worry. These kind people will deliver you to a lovely couple in the south. And don't forget to call your escorts Mama and Papa, as you must pretend to be *their* child on your journey. I would take you myself, but . . ." She stopped herself, not wishing to worry her daughter, and simply enveloped her in one last hug, adding softly, "Remember, I will come for you soon. You, Miriam, Naomi, and I will all be together again."

"But how will you *find* us?" Esther asked, choking back tears.

"Through my connections, darling. I'll know where you and your sisters are at all times. And our apartment will always be home. Don't forget. Because if something happens that makes it impossible for me to come for you, please, go home, as soon as it's safe. Just ask for Mr. Bissett, the property manager, or his wife or children. I gave him our key to safeguard. Everything has been arranged. Will you remember?"

"Yes, Mama. I will. *Je t'aime.*"

"Forever, *ma trésor.*"

And with those words, the woman clutched her heart, then watched her daughter wave goodbye and walk out the door with her escorts. Before leaving the building herself, she pulled a red journal from her pocket and turned to the page that held the information about her two younger daughters. There, she wrote down the real and false names for Esther. Next to that, she wrote the names of the couple who would act as Esther's guardians, along with their location. It was a risk to have all of this information in writing, she knew. But what choice did she have? She was terrible with codes. She was a language teacher, after all, not a mathematician like her late husband. She snapped the book shut and, with every ounce of courage she could muster, she stepped over the threshold and disappeared back into the night.

1

ON THE WAY!

Over the Atlantic
Spring Break, 2013

Jake broke his pencil. The loud snap garnered quick glances from a few of his fellow plane passengers.

"Easy there, Rembrandt," Ben muttered, not looking up from his tablet.

"Ugh!" Jake responded, digging into his backpack for another pencil. "I was really hoping to coast through the second semester of our freshman year. *Why* did I sign up for this art class? I can't draw!"

"I'll tell you why. Because every legendary architect has drafted in pencil and because being able to sketch will help you get to where you want to go." Now Ben looked up and brushed his thick red hair from his eyes.

"Maybe I won't be an architect then," Jake responded.

Ben chuckled. "Jake McGreevy, the 15-year-old who can tell a hip roof from a gambrel roof at a quarter mile won't be an architect? That's rich."

"Why? Because architecture is in my blood?"

"Your dad seems to love it."

"He does, doesn't he? I guess I'll just have to hope that by the time I'm through graduate school, they'll have some sort of brain scan that can transpose my thoughts onto paper."

"Could happen. But meanwhile, maybe one of the street artists in Paris will be able to give you some tips," Ben said.

"If we have time."

"True. We might be pretty busy baking each night for practice." The boys had won a spot as partners in a baking contest for teens at the famed Le Cordon Bleu cooking school in Paris—and the contest would be televised. They still couldn't believe their luck: going to Paris over spring break by themselves! Of course, it wouldn't have been possible unless Ben's aunt, who was living in Paris, had agreed to let them stay with her.

"Plus," Ben said, "we're going to need some time to dig into your mother's past while we're there. It's strange that your dad never looked through her stuff before now."

"Yeah, I think he was just so depressed when she was killed that he couldn't do it. But when I started asking questions after we solved the mystery of her death in Chicago, he showed me all of her boxes."

"Hey, at least he *saved* everything."

"Right, and this has to mean *something*," Jake said, as he pulled a photo out of his backpack's pocket. The tattered black-and-white image featured a woman with two young girls and an infant, standing in front of a window. "This photo was all my mom had left from the house fire that killed her mother—that's what she told my dad. We're pretty sure this photo was taken in Paris, based on the design of the buildings behind them."

"Was your mom's father killed in the fire, too?"

"No. My mom apparently never knew her father."

"Oh! So then what happened to your mom after she lost her mother?" Ben asked.

"She got taken in by a foster family. She was just six years old when it happened, so she apparently didn't have a lot of memories of her mom. But she knew her name, of course: Miriam Charpentier."

"Well, they say a picture is worth a thousand words. I guess we have an essay to write."

"Good thing writing is easier than drawing," Jake said. "At least for me, that is."

*　*　*

The plane's pitch shifted slightly, signaling its descent. Half an hour later, the plane had arrived at the gate at Charles de Gaulle Airport. Ben and Jake pulled their violins from the overhead compartment and made their way through the bustling terminal. Having been so far back in the plane, they found that their luggage was already on the carousel when they arrived at baggage claim. Jake pulled his trusty Leatherman from his suitcase and clipped it to the outside pocket of his backpack. After a brief hold-up in customs, where the agents had to measure the knife blade to confirm it was legal, the boys found their way into the reception area.

"There's my aunt!" Ben pointed and started walking faster.

2
PARIS!

"*Bonjour!*" Ben's Aunt Jenna was in her early 30s and wearing a cowl-neck sweater and leggings with colorful kittens printed on them.

"You've gotten so tall, Ben!" she exclaimed, reaching up to ruffle his hair and give him a big hug. Stepping back, she added, "I know we've seen each other on our tablets, but I guess you were always sitting."

Ben blushed and turned to introduce Jake. "Um, Aunt Jenna, this is my best friend, Jake McGreevy."

Jake extended his hand, but Jenna would have none of that formality. "It is *so* great to finally meet you, Jake!" she exclaimed, enveloping him in a hug. "Ben has told me everything about you!"

"Thank you—same here—and thanks for letting us stay with you," Jake replied.

"My pleasure! Come on, let's go!" Jenna said, grabbing one of Ben's bags and leading the way to the public transportation platform to board the Métro. "We don't want to waste another minute in the airport, do we? We're in Paris!"

Exiting a tunnel and traveling above ground, the train whizzed past famous landmarks and gleaming ornate buildings, all surrounded by a world of spring greenery. Jake swiveled his head like an owl as he tried to process what he was seeing.

"You could get a master's in architecture just by studying one block," he marveled.

"Absolutely!" Jenna replied. "Ben told me about your love of architecture, Jake. I think you've come to the right city. Everywhere you look—arches and gargoyles and flying buttresses."

"Do you ever get tired of it? I mean, does it eventually just become scenery?" Jake asked.

"Not yet for me. Each time I emerge from the Métro, it's like a little jolt of energy," Jenna replied.

"I can't believe you've been here two years now. Other than that one time you came home for Hanukkah, I haven't seen you in so long," Ben said.

"I've missed you, too, Ben," Jenna said, ruffling her nephew's hair again.

Soon enough, they arrived at the station near Jenna's home. A short walk took them to her apartment building, where they followed Jenna into a vintage Otis elevator cab with an old-fashioned manual sliding metal gate.

"Cool! I haven't seen one of these in a long time," Ben said.

"I usually try to take the stairs. This elevator can get stuck sometimes. But with your suitcases and all, we'll just have to risk it," Jenna said, pressing the number 7. The lift lurched to a start but made it without stalling between floors.

"*Mazel tov*, Otis," she said, patting the gate as she slid it open to lead Jake and Ben down the hall.

It was easy to spot her door: it sported a frame in the shape of cat, whose one open eye lined up perfectly with the peep

14

hole. And to the right of that, nailed into her door jamb at an angle, was a cat-adorned mezuzah. *Uh-oh, I'm sensing a theme here,* Jake thought, dragging his suitcase inside.

Although Jenna hadn't impressed Jake as eccentric at the airport, her apartment told a different story. The cat frame and the cat-shaped mezuzah had just been the beginning: the backs of the kitchen chairs were cat-shaped, the tablecloth was adorned with an illustration of a long-haired Persian . . . even the clock was a cat, with its tail a pendulum and its paws pointing to the time.

Don't judge . . . and don't laugh! Everyone has their obsessions, Jake decided, trying to stifle his surprise.

As if on cue, three cats rushed over to greet them.

"How is your PhD coming? What was it in again?" Jake asked, trying not to step on any tails.

"French history, and it's going slow. I thought it would take me 24 months, but I think I have another year of work," Jenna replied. "Now allow me to introduce you to my friends: Cordelia, Puck, and Beatrice. If you see a white cat with beautiful blue eyes, that's Romeo. He doesn't venture out much."

"You're a Shakespeare fan, then?" Jake asked.

"Yes. You like the Bard, too?" she asked.

"Who doesn't?" was all Jake could think to say. Truth was, he didn't love reading old plays, but for some reason, he had a good memory for characters' names.

Jenna showed Jake and Ben the small room they'd be sharing. "Sorry I don't have two beds, but friends have assured me that the air mattress is pretty comfortable."

"It'll be perfect," Ben replied. "Thank you again for having us."

"Oh, and I did the shopping you asked for. I never realized there were so many different kinds of flour, so hopefully I got the right ones."

"Should we practice a few bakes before we try to hunt down someone who might know about the family in the picture?" Ben asked.

"Sounds good to me," Jake said. Just then, he noticed four simple-but-well-done pencil sketches of French landmarks hanging on the wall.

"I like those drawings. Did you do them, Jenna?" Jake asked.

"I did—thank you," she replied.

"I wish I could draw like that."

"It was hard for me at first, but then I took this workshop where you learn to shut off the left side of your brain and allow the right side, the artistic side, to take over," Jenna said.

Jake was intrigued. "Maybe you could show me later?"

"You bet! Listen, I have a few more things to pick up from the store, but feel free to begin baking. *Ma cuisine est ta cuisine*, as they say here in Paris. And Ben, Jake—don't forget to let your folks know that you arrived safe and sound. *Á tout à l'heure!*" When the boys looked at her in confusion, she said, "Toodles, you two!"

* * *

The boys quickly oriented themselves to Aunt Jenna's kitchen and organized the utensils and ingredients into the setup they planned to use for the competition.

"Looks like we have an audience," Ben said, nodding toward the cats watching them.

"Let's hope they don't jump up into our pastry. We don't want furry dough!" Jake joked.

"Right, we want it to be *purr*-fect!"

"*Purr*-haps we'd better get baking, then?" Jake retorted.

"OK, enough cat puns!" Ben laughed.

"*Fur* now," Jake answered. "Sorry, I couldn't resist."

A few hours later, the air was filled with heavenly smells.

The kitchen table overflowed with croissants, apple pie, and a Bakewell tart.

"Yum!" Jenna said, breathing in the welcoming aroma of apples, crust, and jam when she returned from her errands.

"Hope you're hungry!" Ben said.

"I will *definitely* try everything you're serving," Jenna replied. "Maybe I should pack some up for the nursing home."

"Nursing home?" Jake asked.

"I guess I should call it an assisted-living center, as most of the residents don't exactly need nursing. It's a few blocks over. I spend what free time I can there. I know they will flip over your baked goods."

"I volunteer at a place like that in New York," Jake added. *Jenna seems cool. We have a lot in common.*

"We'll have plenty," Ben said. "We'll be baking nonstop while we're here, more than we could ever eat by ourselves."

"Says the man who once inhaled an entire challah," Jake joked.

"More than once, actually. But in this case, I'll try to restrain myself," Ben grinned.

"Tell me about the baking contest," Jenna said, reaching for a warm croissant. "I think I read that it will have a live segment?"

"Right. Well, as Ben told you, it's being held at Le Cordon Bleu culinary school. There will be eight teams from various countries. One bake will be taped each morning for five days and then edited to be aired the following night. After each bake, one team will get eliminated. After the fifth day, assuming we are still in the competition, there will be a live show that will feature the three remaining teams. Here's the schedule," Jake said, handing Jenna a chart.

"OK, let's clean up and head out," Ben said. "It might take us a while to find the apartment building in your mother's photo."

Moments later, Jake and Ben were striding beside the River Seine, which was shimmering in the rays of the afternoon sun.

Gray marble buildings with embellished rock archways lined the river on the near side. Across the waterway, Jake could see similarly elaborate structures, with the Eiffel Tower rising above them all, like a noble sentry guarding its charges. Several moored houseboats rocked gently against the walls at the river's edge, creating a rhythmic, peaceful splashing.

"Paris, Ben. We're in Paris!" Jake exclaimed. "Can you believe it? History, architecture, art . . . and look at that architecture!" Jake's head swept back and forth.

"You said architecture twice," Ben snickered.

Jake ignored him. "I'm glad we got into the competition so we could come here."

"Well, your fame from Ireland and Chicago makes you a great human-interest story for this contest," Ben commented, referring to Jake's earlier adventures. "How many people our age can say they found a hidden treasure or solved the mystery of their mother's death? That's probably one of the reasons the director picked us."

"Well, anyway, you should say *our* fame, Ben," Jake said.

"Right, well . . . I'm just glad we *might* get coaching from François Marquette. I've heard he can be tough to please, but he's one of the top bakers in the *world!*"

"Your baking chores at Stanley House Arts Camp really sparked something in you, didn't they?" Jake said.

"Yeah, since our winter break in Chicago, I haven't been able to stop."

"Ben, are you worried at all about what everybody back at school will think when they see us on TV *baking?*"

"I was, a little, at first. But then I thought, who cares? As people say, you've gotta let it go. Life's too short to worry about what other people think." Ben pointed to the Métro entrance and the boys descended the stairs. After a quick consult of the map, they found themselves on the train headed toward the 20th *arrondissement.*

3

MERCI BEAUCOUP

"How are you going to do this? Wander around the square, asking if people are related to you?" Ben asked, squeezing the overhead rail tighter as the crowded train car rocked back and forth.

"Slightly more scientific than that, but basically, yes," Jake chuckled, as he maneuvered himself to pull the old photograph from his backpack.

"See that view through the window behind the family?" Jake pointed at the image.

"Yes, looks like a church."

"Not just any church. That's the Église Notre-Dame-de-la-Croix de Ménilmontant."

"Those spires don't look like Notre-Dame," Ben commented.

"Different cathedral than the famous Notre-Dame. This one was built much later, during the 19th century, in Gothic Revival. That's how I was able to narrow the location down to Paris. When my dad and I saw the picture, he knew it was Gothic Revival architecture. So we googled cathedrals of that style and scanned pictures till we matched it to the photo. Based on the perspective, we realized the apartment must be on a street called Rue de Ménilmontant."

"Say *that* street name three times fast," Ben said.

Jake laughed after he tried and failed. "So, ready to go knock on some doors?"

"Sure. I just hope someone can identify the people in your photo," Ben said.

"Me, too. Who knows. If this family kept their apartment or left it to relatives . . ." Jake's words caught in his throat as he led Ben up the Métro station steps.

"I know. It will be pretty amazing if this works," Ben said. "Sort of like one of those crime shows, but instead of fancy computers checking algorithms of sun shadows, you used your architecture knowledge and internet photos to match it up. You're a wonder, McGreevy." Ben patted Jake on the back.

"Wonder . . . or biggest time-waster ever."

*   *   *

On reaching the cathedral, Jake spun around several times. "There, that must be the building!" Jake pointed to an apartment building across the street. "Let's start on the top floor and work our way down. From the photo, it looks like they're pretty high off the ground."

Full of energy now, the boys crossed the street and rushed up the stairs to the fifth floor of the building. They approached the first door, number 502, and knocked gently.

"I have to remember to breathe. I'm too nervous—or excited," Jake said.

"Probably both," Ben replied.

Silence.

Jake knocked again, a bit louder.

"Buzzkill. Nobody's home," Ben said. "Could be at work."

"Right. Mark the apartment down as a no-show in case we need to come back later," Jake suggested.

"Got it." Ben flipped his trusty tablet computer to note mode and scribbled on the screen with a digital pen.

Jake knocked on the adjacent apartment door and was rewarded with the sound of footsteps.

"Good sign," Ben said.

"*Bonjour?*" A gentleman around 50 years old opened the door.

"*Bonjour. Parlez-vous Anglais?*" Jake stammered.

"*Oui*, yes, how can I help?" The man replied in perfect English.

"I am looking for the family in this picture. I think it is from a long time ago, but it was taken in this building." Jake held up the photograph, and the man leaned forward and peered at it.

"It does look like this building. The window style in my apartment is exactly the same. Wait a minute. There *is* a woman in this building who grew up here before the war. She and her granddaughter live in apartment 408. Perhaps your answer lies right below me on the fourth floor."

Jake started to tremble. "Thank you! I mean, *merci—merci beaucoup*, sir," he said, pumping the man's hand vigorously.

"Yes, *merci* very much!" Ben said, pulling Jake away.

*   *   *

"Apartment 408." Jake's voice quivered as he stood in front of the door.

"Are you planning to knock or what?" Ben asked.

"Yes, of course. I'm just trying to calm down first."

"*Shpilkes*," Ben muttered.

"Translate?"

"Yiddish for 'pins and needles,' what you have when you're nervous," Ben replied.

"*Shpilkes* indeed." Jake knocked. To the boys' relief, a girl around 15 years old answered the door. She was slightly taller than Jake and had thick sandy-blonde hair, like his. She looked at them with a slightly puzzled air, idly twisting

was taken here." Jake gently placed the old photograph in the woman's lined hands.

Within seconds, tears rolled down her cheeks. After a moment, the woman dabbed her eyes and rose from her chair. Jake and the girl both reached out to assist.

"Come with me, please." Her soft French accent was laced with emotion. She led them to a buffet across the room and pulled open the center drawer, extracting an envelope and pulling a picture out of its protective sleeve. She carefully laid Jake's photo and her own side by side.

They were identical.

"Is this your family?" Jake asked the woman.

"*Oui*. This is my mother, Dahlia, and this one is me when I was nine," she said, pointing to the taller girl. "That is my younger sister. She was five. And this is our baby sister, two years old," she said, lightly tapping the images of her sisters. "This picture was taken in January of 1940, here in Paris, a couple of years before the worst began."

"The worst?" Ben asked.

"*Oui*, when the deportations started. Before that, sensing doom, my mother had sent my younger sisters away at the first opportunity—Miriam, in June 1940 and Naomi in January 1941—through special arrangements she made with other families. I knew nothing about those plans. Then it was my turn. It was early July 1942. We had been in hiding by then for a month. It was so difficult for us without Papa, who had died serving in the French army two years before. I had resisted leaving my mother for over a year. But when it became even more dangerous, she arranged false identification papers for me and the two escorts who posed as my parents for the journey south. One moment I was in hiding in Paris, and the next I was on a farm in the south of France. Though I was safer, I was not free. Living on a remote farm

25

under a false name only meant that the police weren't *likely* to find me."

Jake was so engrossed in the older woman's story that he had to replay the name he'd heard her say just a moment before. "Wait—Miriam? Is that what you said?"

"*Oui.* Miriam."

"But that—that was my grandmother's name!" Jake gasped.

The woman put her hand to her heart. "*Mon dieu*, could it be? *Impossible.* This must be a dream."

Jake stared at the photo in his hands.

Seeing the sudden strain on her grandmother's face, the girl said, "Bubbe, we should have some tea, don't you think?" She ushered them all to the table and then went to put on the kettle.

"I apologize," Jake said. "This is a shock. And we didn't even introduce ourselves. I'm Jake McGreevy and this is my best friend, Ben Meyers."

"I am Sophie Lévy, and this is my grandmother, Esther Shneyer." They all shook hands, then sat down at the kitchen table.

Esther examined Jake, looking for a family resemblance. "Your hair and eyes—they are so much like my Sophie's," she said.

Jake blushed and asked her to start at the beginning.

"Where to start? You boys know about the Nazis and what they did to the Jewish people, *oui?*" Esther asked.

"Very much so," Ben answered, his voice cracking. "My grandfather is a survivor."

"Ah." The woman nodded, patting his hand.

Sophie set down a plate of rugelach—a sweet rolled pastry filled with chocolate—and poured out the cups of tea. Jake took a sip. His mind registered the tea as terribly hot, but he was so disoriented, he didn't recoil. All he could think was,

I can't believe I'm here with my grandmother's sister!

"*Les années noires*. The dark years," Esther began. "The Germans had already invaded Denmark, Norway, Belgium, and Poland—the country of my parents' birth. Then France surrendered in June 1940. Over the next two years, our lives became more restricted and unsettling. Things we take for granted today—freedom of movement, bicycles, radios, phones, financial security—all were taken away. The word 'Juif,' *Jew*, was stamped in red on our identity cards and in our ration books. I don't know how my mother anticipated it, but she seemed to know that things would keep getting worse, and that is why she sent my sisters away very soon after the German Occupation. She was right, too. The Germans bombed our synagogue. We lived in fear of roundups and deportations. Then in June 1942, almost two years after we had been required by the French police, under German orders, to register for the census, Jews were forced to sew a yellow Star of David badge onto the left side of their outermost piece of clothing. I remember that it was large with a black border and the word 'Juif' in black inscribed across it. That's when many of our people left Paris for the south. Others, like my mother and me, went into hiding. We didn't just disappear, though—or, at least, my mother didn't. Since March, as Jews were fleeing after the deportation, she'd been working to safeguard their possessions. You see, that month, Hitler had ordered the looting of apartments that Jews had once lived in—Jews who had fled or been deported or arrested. The Nazis stole small things, like dishes and bed linens, and big items, too—those that were *important* to families. What is the word?" She looked at Sophie for help.

"Heirlooms, maybe?" Ben offered.

"Yes, heirlooms, anything of value."

"But why did they steal such insignificant items like linens?" Jake asked.

"My mother said the Nazis did that to *erase* us. They were also emptying museums of treasures. So my mother's group hid small items, like paintings and photographs—and large pieces, like pianos and furniture, such as our beloved *horloge comtoise—*"

"What you call a grandfather clock," Sophie translated.

Her grandmother nodded. "She wrote everything down in a journal—a blue book. I remember that it had a strap with a square brass tip that clicked into a clasp on the top in the shape of a scroll. I recall peeking at it once. There were so many names of people and their possessions. I offered to help—I was already 11 years old, so not such a child anymore, as I told her. But she wanted me to stay hidden."

"How did they move all of these items?" Ben asked.

"Ah, how to transport things without the evil eyes of the French police and the Nazis noticing? But my mother did not only transport *things.*"

The boys' rapt attention urged her to continue.

"After the arrest of over a thousand Jews in March 1942 and their deportation to Auschwitz, my mother began helping people with arrangements to leave the city and then to leave France altogether. Her group also helped children who were traveling alone to the border of the Free Zone in the south. I offered her every reason I could think of why I should stay with her. But then one day, she sat me down and said, 'Esther, it's time. You need to leave . . . now. I will stay in hiding so that I can continue to help our people, and you will live with a family far away from here.' I was upset, *naturellement.* I was confused, too. I wanted my mother to come with me. I didn't want to accept this reality. Losing my papa had been excruciating. Not having my sisters with me—not knowing where they were—was terrible in a different way. So the thought of being separated from my mother was simply unbearable."

Sophie placed her hand on her grandmother's arm.

"I asked her, 'Mama, how will we find each other after the war?' And she said, 'I will come for you. I know where your sisters are, and I know where you're going.'"

Sophie helped her grandmother reach the teacup in front of her. Esther took a few sips before continuing.

"But we never did . . . reunite, you understand. Suffice it to say, thanks to my mother's foresight, I was fortunate to be able to come back home and I continued to live here with the eldest daughter of the farm family who took me in. She left when I married at the age of 20, and I've been here ever since. I prayed that someday I would hear a knock on my door. That door," she said, wagging her finger, "has been silent for 68 years. But then, you appeared. You are the first clue in nearly seven long decades that at least one of my sisters lived! Little Miriam!"

Jake's throat tightened and tears coursed down his cheeks. The gravity of the moment made everyone silent.

"Jake, can you tell us about yourself and your mother and Miriam?" Sophie finally suggested.

Jake wiped his cheeks with his sleeve. "My mother died when I was two years old. She was murdered in Chicago after uncovering a massive art scandal. I learned from my father that my mom's mother, Miriam, had come from Europe in the 1950s, but he didn't know much else except that Miriam had died in a fire when my mother was six. My mother never knew her father. This photo was all she had left of her mother's possessions. It had been in a safe in her bedroom closet."

Sophie frowned. "That is *très tragique*," she said, encircling her grandmother in a hug.

"Yes, I know. I'm so sorry." Jake cleared his throat gently. "I need to ask you a question about this. May I?"

"Of course," Esther said, trying to regain her composure.

"See here? There's some writing on the back. Do you know what it means? We translated it, but Ben and I can't figure out what it's really trying to say."

Sophie turned the picture over: "*Notre endroit préféré a un grand trésor.*" She looked up, puzzled. "Our picture has that writing, too. It means, 'Our favorite place has a great treasure.'"

"Yes, but it sounds like a riddle, doesn't it?" Jake said. "Like something is hidden there."

"*Mon dieu!*" Esther threw her hands up in the air and fell back into her chair. "How could I have missed it! Yes, of course—it *is* a riddle. I had thought all these years that it was just a poorly worded reminder to 'treasure our favorite places—something my mother had written hurriedly before sending me off. But now that I know Miriam's photo has these words as well, it must be a riddle," she explained. "My mother *loved* to entertain us with those! Oy, how could I have missed this?"

"Well, don't worry. It isn't too late. And Ben and I have some experience hunting down clues," Jake said, resting his hand on Ben's shoulder.

"Perhaps it refers to the blue book with the families' names and the list of their valuables? Or it could be where the possessions are actually hidden," Sophie said.

"Hopefully both," Jake replied, "so we can get them into their rightful owners' hands."

"Bubbe, do you remember where your family liked to go?" Sophie asked. "Their favorite places, I mean."

"Oh, yes. We loved the grotto at the Buttes-Chaumont Park." A bright smile lit up her face as she imagined the picturesque cave she had visited in her youth. "I haven't been there in years." She paused, but then with a vigor she hadn't displayed before, added, "We should go!"

"Great!" Jake said. "When?"

"Why not now?" Esther replied. Sophie looked surprised for a moment, then sprang into action and pulled her grandmother's walker from a closet. The foursome took the elevator to the ground floor. Esther turned her walker toward the Métro entrance, but before she could take a step, Jake put a hand on her arm to stop her.

"Please, allow me," he said quietly, and hailed a cab. Although Sophie said nothing, Jake sensed that she was relieved to spare her grandmother the walk through the crowded train stations.

5

A REAL GEM

The cab took them through the city toward the northeast part of Paris and dropped them at their destination: the pedestrian entrance to the Parc des Buttes Chaumont.

Demonstrating impressive stamina and drive, Esther trudged nearly 400 feet into the park toward an artificial lake with an island at its center.

"Wow, I had no idea this was even here. It's not featured in my guidebook," Ben marveled.

"We Parisians like to keep *some* things for ourselves," Sophie said with a wink. It was the first light-hearted comment they'd heard her make since they'd met.

Jake remained silent as he took in the scene. Dominating the landscape was a miniature Roman-style temple, situated high on the cliffs of a small island. *What a fantastic view you could get from there*, he thought.

"Qu'est-ce que c'est?" Esther said, as she approached one of the two bridges that connected the park to the island. A large chain-link fence blocked their entry.

"Looks like this area is under construction," Ben said.

Jake scanned the area. "Doesn't seem like an active site to *me*; and we won't *disturb* anything." He pulled on the chain that fastened the fence gate together. "We should be able to get through here. Might need to help your grandmother balance as she ducks under the chain, though."

"*Arrêtez!*" A loud voice called out. An electric golf cart sped toward them and came skidding to a stop. Two dark-haired men dressed in guard uniforms jumped out. One was tall and heavyset and the other was short and wiry. The badges on their uniforms sported their names: Pierre was the larger man; Michel, the smaller.

Sophie smiled at the guards, twisting her Star of David pendant. "*Est-il possible de visiter l'île?*" she asked. "Is it possible to visit the island?" But the guards didn't return her smile. Instead, the larger guard shouted something at her, and Sophie and Esther recoiled as one, as if his words had hit them in the face.

Pierre then unlocked the chain, wrapped it even tighter around the fence, relocked it, and stood with his arms folded over his chest as Michel attached a new sign to the fence, written in French and English: *En cours de construction. Accès interdit.* Under construction. No trespassing.

Dejected, Sophie helped turn her grandmother's walker around, and they all trudged back toward the park's entrance.

"What did that guard say?" Jake whispered to Sophie.

"I don't want to repeat it," she said, clutching her Star of David pendant, "but it was *antisémitique*, an insult to Jewish people." A tear rolled down her cheek.

Jake's throat tightened and he turned back to look at the guards, balling his fist.

"Come on. I know what you're thinking," Ben said, ushering Jake away from the park. "We can't fight them—not this way."

* * *

Back at the apartment, Ben connected his tablet to the Wi-Fi. "It says here that the temple and the grotto on the island—and the two bridges spanning the lake to the island—are all closed. Those areas will be under construction to upgrade the drainage, sidewalks, and bridges for the next—get this—*two* years!"

"But we can't wait two years!" Sophie glanced at her grandmother.

"Agreed." Jake nodded. "Maybe you could call the construction company in the morning. I'm sure they will let us in when they hear what we're looking for. Ben and I are actually here for an international baking contest and we won't be free until noon, but we'll come right over afterwards, okay?"

"Yes, *parfait*. That sounds perfect. This has been an amazing day. *Merci beaucoup* . . . thank you for finding us," Sophie said, swiftly enveloping Jake and Ben in a tight embrace.

6

HEATHER AND BAKE 1

"Thirty seconds, everyone. This is your last chance to make everything *egg*-cellent," Jacques, the baking show's master of ceremonies, joked.

"Our host likes puns!" Ben whispered.

Jake didn't hear Jacques *or* Ben. All he could say was, "Orange sauce or blueberry?"

"Orange?" Ben said, questioningly.

"We've got one shot to get this right. Orange or blue?" Jake's voice was strained.

"Definitely orange," Ben responded.

Jake's hands flashed across the table.

"Time!" Jacques bellowed, and the two boys stepped back from the table. Jake drew a breath, his first in what felt like forever, as the two judges approached.

"What do we have here, *messieurs?*" François, the tall, thin chef-turned-judge inquired in a thick accent. He was dressed in a starch-white baker's jacket, which stood out against his voluminous chestnut hair.

"White chocolate and raspberry cheesecake with orange sauce on the side, sir." Somehow, Ben seemed taller than his six feet as he responded. *Good for Ben. He's really in his element,* Jake thought.

"White chocolate can be difficult. We shall see if you tempered it enough to have the flavor come through," François said.

"I think it looks superb," the second judge countered. Meredith was a woman in her 50s with a British accent, and her colorful skirt and cardigan were a stark contrast to François's attire. "Clear definition between the crust and the cheesecake and just the right amount of fruit on top."

They're probably dressed differently to provide some visual interest for the cameras, Jake thought. He tried not to look at the cameraman zooming in on their dessert plate.

The French judge picked up a silver fork, squared off a piece of the cheesecake, and then peered at it as if it were a specimen in a petri dish. He took a bite.

Jake held his breath. He could feel heat radiating from Ben.

"Acceptable," the chef deadpanned.

"Oh, I think it's *much* more than acceptable. It's scrumptious! Brilliant visual presentation, distinct flavors, and a clean finish. Well done, boys," Meredith cheered.

Light applause emanated from the other contestants, who were standing beside their desserts, eagerly awaiting their own appraisals. The two judges, with camera crew in tow, traveled slowly from table to table, while Jake and Ben waited in agony for the first day's results.

*   *   *

"Unfortunately, our Egyptian friends will not be coming back on day 2," Meredith announced a short time later, after her conference with François. "We do wish them well on their culinary journey," she added, as she and François hugged them goodbye.

"A-a-and cut!" the director called.

"OK, buddy, well done! We landed in the middle of the

pack." Jake gave Ben a quick half-hug, like football players after a score.

"I was worried the orange sauce would make it too tart," Ben critiqued himself.

"It was spot on, and I think the British judge likes things with bold flavors," Jake replied. "Besides, we don't need to be first each day. We just need to not be last! Now let's clean up and get out of here." Jake grabbed a rag and started brushing the crumbs from their workstation. As he swept some powder into his hands, his nose twitched.

"*Aaachhooo!*" The powerful sneeze blew flour off the table in a great puff.

"*Oi!* Watch it!" A well-dressed girl scolded him in a British accent. She looked older than Jake but was about his height and wore a white scarf around her dark ponytail.

"I'm so sorry, ugh, um . . . !" Jake went to brush the flour from her skirt but then pulled his hand back, recognizing the awkwardness of the situation. "Seems as though they just threw us into baking and filming right away without any introductions. I'm Jake McGreevy and this is my baking partner and best friend, Ben Meyers." Jake dusted his hand off on his pants and extended it.

"Heather Baker. No jokes please." The girl ignored Jake's hand and continued to dust herself off.

"Where's your partner?" Jake gestured to the other baking stations, all manned by a pair of teens.

"I don't need one," she answered curtly.

"Oh, I see. Well, sorry . . . again." Jake turned away and resumed his cleaning.

"No, *I'm* sorry. That was so rude," Heather said. "I'm just incredibly focused on this contest." Her voice softened. "I have to win. It will be expected, given my father's reputation."

"Wait a minute! Heather Baker. Is your dad *Oliver* Baker,

the head pastry chef at Buckingham Palace?" Ben asked.

"Yes, how—"

"I read about him online last month. And there was a picture of your family at home in your kitchen. Jake, Oliver Baker is both the youngest pastry chef ever to supervise the kitchen at the palace and the first Black man to serve in that position. They call him 'the Man with the Golden Whisk, meticulous in every detail and confident in his flavors,'" Ben said, recalling a quote from the article.

"You forgot to mention the high standards he holds everyone else to," Heather lamented.

"Sorry," Ben said. "That sounds rough."

"Well, at least desserts at your house are probably always worth waiting for!" Jake said, trying to lighten the mood.

"That's true." Heather laughed a little. "You actually haven't lived until you've tried my dad's chocolate cake."

"Next stop, London!" Ben said, high-fiving Jake.

"You have to know that chocolate cake is, well, our favorite dessert. In fact—" Jake was going to tell Heather all about the outstanding chocolate cake they had made in Chicago but was interrupted by Jacques, who called for everyone's attention.

"Well done today, contestants!" Jacques announced. "Tomorrow—well, let's just say that we're going to get to the *meat* of the matter." The corner of his mouth curled a bit and his eyes danced.

And with that, the director ushered all the contestants out the door.

Ben had made a point to walk beside Heather and now continued their earlier conversation. "Is his whisk really made of gold?"

"No, it's just colored gold. He received it as a gag gift when he was starting out, but he liked it, and he considers it his lucky charm. He even has a special case for it," Heather said.

"That's cool. I love stories like that," Ben said.

Looking up from his phone, Jake grabbed Ben's arm and said, "Sorry, but we have to go, Heather. See you tomorrow!"

"Sure, I'll—" But before she could finish her sentence, they were off. She gave a short wave to no one in particular and walked in the opposite direction.

"Wasn't that a little abrupt?" Ben said.

"Yeah, I guess it was. I'll apologize tomorrow. But Ben, we're late getting to Sophie's, and I *really* want to figure out how to see inside that part of the park that's off limits, in case the construction company rejected Sophie's request."

"Got it," Ben said.

They picked up their pace as they ran down the wide stone stairs of the Métro station. Once they found their seats on the train, Jake relaxed and pulled a piece of paper from his backpack to show Ben.

"What do you think?"

"I think tomorrow we're going to be making a meat pie," Ben said, looking at his tablet.

"Oh, because Jacques said, 'Meat of the matter'?"

"Yes!" Ben answered.

"OK, but what I was asking about was this—my drawing. Jenna gave me some tips on how to silence my left brain. I think it helped a little."

"This is great!" Ben replied. "Really, I mean it, Jake. I recognize it—it's the Arc de Triomphe, right?"

"Right. To keep my left brain from overpowering the right, I said the name of each part of the building aloud. That way, my hand could be driven by the right side uninterrupted!" Jake felt his phone buzz. "I'm getting a text." He pulled his phone from his pocket.

"It's Sophie. She's been picked up by the police!"

7

CHEVY

"She wants us to come get her at the police station. She gave me the address—it's in the 19th *arrondissement*. She must have gone to the park again and gotten caught by the guards. Why else would she be in the 19th *arrondissement* jurisdiction?" Jake muttered.

"Wish she had waited for *us*," Ben replied.

"I get the sense she's pretty independent. Did you notice that only she and her grandmother live in the apartment? I think she's basically on her own. We didn't actually ask her, but she never mentioned her parents, did she?"

A flash of color caught Jake's eye as the boys climbed into their Peugeot taxicab. A red-helmeted rider on a beat-up white moped was parked 50 yards away. The moped rider gunned the bike's throttle and sped past the boys.

"Earth to Jake," Ben said.

"Sorry!" Jake shook his head. "I just got one of those weird feelings."

Their cab driver navigated in fits and starts through the midday traffic, giving both boys a little whiplash, and finally arrived at an ordinary-looking building: gray stone with a simple glass door, engraved with the words *Police Nationale*.

"Definitely not like the movies. No impressive staircase or

hum of activity," Ben said as he held the door open for Jake.

"No, it seems more like a dentist's office than a police station," Jake said.

Inside, a deskbound policeman sat in command of the reception area, which was sparsely decorated with plants, chairs, and a magazine-covered coffee table.

"*Bonjour*, or should I say, hello?" the man said.

"How did you know we spoke English?" Jake asked.

"I am a *policier*. You think I cannot spot an American from three meters?"

Need to make a friend here, Jake thought. "*Touché*," he grinned, using the last of his French. "We're looking for a friend of ours. A girl named Sophie."

"*Oui*, we've been expecting you." The policeman stood and motioned for Jake and Ben to follow him through a large wooden door, which opened onto cubicle offices and a holding cell in the far corner. Another hallway farther back presumably led to more offices. The policeman brought them to a small conference room and announced, "*Lieutenant, les Americains sont ici.*"

Standing in the room, glaring coldly and with arms folded, stood the two guards from the park. A bald man with an unbuttoned jacket stood next to them. Jake could see a badge hanging from the man's belt.

Directly across, sitting motionless in a chair at the center of the table, was Sophie. Her eyes, red and teary, seemed to beg for help when Jake looked at her. Another officer, shorter and more athletic-looking than his bald colleague, stood behind her. He too had a badge on his belt, but unlike the bald officer, he had a compassionate look on his face.

This man nodded and motioned for Jake and Ben to come closer. "I am Lieutenant Chevrolet."

Jake tried to suppress his eyebrow from rising.

"*Oui*, like the car company." The man's smile was so disarming that Jake relaxed for the first time since entering the building.

"We want this girl arrested!" the tall guard bellowed. "And you might as well send these two back to America. They are equally guilty."

"*Messieurs*," the lieutenant said calmly. "*Bien sûr*, of course, she should not have been there. But if we arrest every person who wanders into a park or a construction site without authorization, we will cripple the courts. Now, I have listened to her story. I don't see why you can't just escort her and her friends to the island. They won't be there long and then they will stop bothering you. Am I right?"

"Absolutely," Jake said. *I like this guy,* he thought. *And I'll bet his friends call him Chevy.* "We just need a little time to look for a possible clue about the location of some Jewish people's possessions from the 1940s—things that were hidden for safekeeping when the Nazis occupied Paris."

"I'm sorry, *monsieur*. We do not get to pick and choose what laws we enforce. The law is the law. You have no right to trespass, no matter how noble your intentions." The bald officer spoke with an impassioned yet elegant tone.

Jake's eyes bounced back and forth like ping-pong balls between Chevy and his colleague. *I think we've stepped into some sort of power struggle here.*

Fueled by their new ally, one of the park's guards pointed at Sophie. "I can see it in her eyes. She will not let this go. You should just arrest her now and save us all the time and aggravation."

"*Que se passe-t-il?*" a voice boomed from the doorway. Chevy and the bald detective immediately stiffened.

"*Capitaine*, we are just discussing a trespassing case," Chevy said in English.

42

The captain, who filled the door with his physical presence, looked Jake and Ben over. "Americans?"

"*Oui,*" Chevy replied.

"Are the Americans the offenders?"

"No," Chevy replied.

"*Oui,*" the bald detective said simultaneously. The captain raised an eyebrow.

"Well, not technically," Chevy replied. "Their friend, this *jeune fille,* was apprehended at the construction site at the Parc des Buttes Chaumont."

"I see. But why does it take two of my detectives to handle a trespassing case? Have we already solved all of the *other* crimes in Paris today?" The captain scowled at the men.

"It's complicated," Chevy replied and continued to explain the situation.

The captain turned to the bald policeman. "Lieutenant Boucher, I assume you want them arrested—letter of the law?" he said.

"*Oui. Le chantier de construction est dangereux. Nous devons montrer l'exemple pour ne plus avoir d'intrusions.*"

Everyone else is speaking English, but he answers in French. Not very inclusive, Jake thought.

The captain locked eyes with his two detectives. "Let them go." He looked at Sophie. "If you or your American friends are caught again, I'll send *them* home immediately, and *you* will be arrested."

Turning on his heels, the captain left the conference room as abruptly as he'd entered. A moment later—not fast enough for any of them—Sophie, Jake, and Ben were out on the street. "What did he say?" Ben asked Sophie at once.

"That it was a dangerous construction site and no more trespassing should happen," Sophie replied. "They also wanted to set an example by arresting me."

As the three spoke on the sidewalk, the station door opened behind them and Lieutenant Chevrolet stepped out. "*Bon*, you are still here . . ."

8

YOU'LL HELP US?

Joining their circle, he began, "Please know that I am sympathetic to your cause. I come from a long line of policemen, you see. My great-grandfather, my grandfather, and my father all served our grand city. But the police have not always done right by the French people. *Par example*, too many of them collaborated with the Nazis. My grandfather was one of the few who stood up to the Germans back then. How could I tarnish his memory by turning my back on you now?" he said.

"So you'll *help* us?" Jake asked.

"As much as I can. *Oui.* I am afraid that will not be much, though. I haven't the right or the ability to gain access to the island in the park. But I will try to think of something. Believe me."

"Lieutenant Chevrolet, who was that other detective?" Jake asked.

"*S'il vous plaît*, call me Chevy. Please. That's what my friends call me."

I knew it, Jake smiled. "Thank you, . . . Chevy."

"The other detective is Boucher. He's not really a bad sort—he's just too ambitious for my taste. Plus he is always a—what is the English expression for *exact*?"

"Stickler?" Jake offered.

"*Oui.* He is a stickler for the law. He enforces what is written without taking the circumstances into account. It has gotten worse since the captain announced his retirement," Chevy finished.

"So Boucher wants to be the new captain?" Ben asked.

"He wants to be king, if you ask me. But since the French monarchy ended with the Revolution, he'll settle for *Directeur Générale* of the police." Chevy pulled several business cards out of his pocket and handed them to the kids. "Text me your phone numbers so I can find you. If you need anything, please call me. I wish you well. Meanwhile, I will, as you say, put my 'thinking cap' on."

They all watched wordlessly as Chevy bounded up the stairs and disappeared back into the station.

Walking toward the Métro, Sophie finally broke the silence. "Thank you so much for coming down here. I didn't know who else to call. I couldn't call my Bubbe, obviously. When the guards started describing you to the police, I don't know why, but something in the expression on Chevy's face gave me the impression that he could be trusted, so I told him I'd text you to come down here."

"You guessed right. Seems like he might be a valuable friend," Jake replied.

"I just didn't want you to think I turned on you . . ." Sophie seemed to shrink a bit.

"Not at all! We're all in this together," Ben said.

"Is school out for spring break here as well, or did you take today off?" Jake asked.

"Sort of both. I'm on a self-paced program," she replied.

"So you don't go to class or anything?" Jake asked.

"I'm finished with regular high school classes and I am taking some beginning college courses and helping Bubbe out."

"I'm confused. I thought you were like 15 or something?" Ben said.

"Yes, I am 15. But I have near-perfect memory recall—some would call it a photographic memory. I learn very quickly. I live with Bubbe because it's closer to the university and because she needs help but has always refused to leave the apartment in case her sisters came home to search for her. My parents live a few blocks away, so I still see them a lot, although right now they are volunteering with Doctors without Borders in Algeria."

"Algeria, why there?" Ben asked.

"The Algerians need medical care, and since it used to be a French colony, a lot of the population speaks French," Sophie replied.

"Wow. That's pretty cool," Jake said. *The world needs more selfless people like them*, he thought.

"Yes, but I wish they were here now. My father has that convincing doctor's voice that could have helped me with the construction company today," Sophie lamented.

"So, no chance of their letting us into the grotto on the island?" Jake asked.

"No. I called the company twice and they were firm in their answer. They said if they paused construction for every potential impact on history, nothing in this town would ever get built," she replied.

"Not that I agree, at least not in this instance, but they have a point," Jake said softly. "Every building in this city is older than our country! How could you ever upgrade anything without demolishing something from the past?"

"But they should have at least let us walk around. It's not like this is some secret government site they're building. They're upgrading a public park for people to walk in, for Pete's sake," Ben stammered.

47

Boy, he's taking this personally. Jake put his hand on his friend's shoulder, then paused.

"What is it?" Ben asked.

Jake nodded to a moped parked farther down the block. "I think I saw that moped when we came out of the baking contest."

"The same one? There have to be a thousand like it in this city," Ben replied.

"Actually, there are 460,000 motorcycles and mopeds in Paris. So probably closer to 3,000 of that model," Sophie corrected him.

Photographic memory indeed, Jake thought. "Yeah, probably. Just got a weird feeling. Anyway, I've got an idea about the grotto. Do you think you could do some shopping in the morning while we're at the baking contest? You'll need to go to a few different stores." Jake handed Sophie his credit card and texted her a list of supplies.

*   *   *

"Well, Aunt Jenna, we just had an interesting experience," Ben said as the boys entered her apartment.

"And he's not *kitten* around, either!" Jake couldn't resist but felt bad about the pun when Ben glared in his direction. The boys filled Jenna in on Sophie, her grandmother, Dahlia, and the police station as she put the finishing touches on their meal.

"Do your PhD classes cover stuff like World War II?" Ben asked.

"No, my focus is on Napoleonic history—the time from 1799 to 1815. But on my own, I've been reading about the 20th century. A benefit of my time at the assisted-living home is access to people who actually lived through what most of us can only study in textbooks. The stories some of them tell are pretty amazing." She doled out the pasta-vegetable-cashew concoction she had prepared onto plates.

"I know," Jake said. "Now that you mention it, a new resident at the place where I volunteer, a Jewish man, started to tell me a lot about his life. Just as he was describing his childhood in Warsaw, he got pulled into a game of bridge. Then we came to France, so . . ."

"You never told me that," Ben said.

"Wasn't much to tell."

"So anyway, I'm guessing, based on what you've already told me, you want to know about the French Resistance?" Jenna said.

"I know they sabotaged equipment and train tracks, but did they do anything to safeguard valuables? Specifically, did they try to protect the Jews' possessions?" Jake asked.

"Oh, absolutely. In fact, one of the most honored members of the Resistance was a French art historian named Rose Valland. Have you ever heard of her? You'll be interested to know this, Jake; she was also a high school drawing teacher. She helped to secretly document *thousands* of stolen works of art and noted where they were being sent. The Nazis would have killed her if they'd discovered what she was doing with the French Resistance. Without her information, so many treasures would have never been recovered!"

"Incredible!" Ben said, typing "Rose Valland" into his tablet. "What about other possessions?"

"Well, I have to assume there were also others hiding treasures from the Nazis," Jenna replied.

"So it's plausible that Dahlia was helping to safeguard them," Jake concluded.

"Oh, most definitely," Jenna replied.

* * *

After they finished dinner, topped off by a delicious apple tart, Jake telephoned his father. Then he brushed his teeth and joined Ben, who was already in their bedroom.

"What I wonder," Jake said, "is what happened to my great-grandmother Dahlia? Why didn't she survive?"

"I don't know. Could be lots of reasons. Everyone from that time has their own story. Maybe we can help tell Dahlia's." Ben pulled a blanket with a tiger's face over himself. "Get some sleep, Jake."

Clearly, she sacrificed herself somehow, Jake thought. *And she never saw her children again. I have that in common with Esther: we both had mothers who, while doing the right thing, risked it all. Of course, they wanted to live, to see their children again, but . . .* "You're right, Ben. Everyone *does* have their own story, but many will never be told. It's like a giant puzzle with permanently missing pieces. But those heirlooms and that blue book—they're going to help a lot. All we have to do now is find them!"

9

THE GROTTO AND BAKE 2

"Bonjour, bakers. This morning, you will bake a meat pie. The choice of crust or filling is yours, and it must be ready for us to taste in two hours," Jacques explained. "As usual, you will find everything you need in the refrigerators and in the supply cabinets and drawers."

"You were right, Ben—it's a meat pie!" Jake whisper-yelled.

"Well, on a scale of 1 to 10, his pun rated a 1 for difficulty, so I can't take too much credit," he said, brushing off imaginary crumbs from his shoulders. "Anyway, I've been thinking about it since yesterday. How about we go with a chicken pot pie?" Ben asked.

"Sounds all-American and delicious to me," Jake said. "I've been feeling a little homesick."

"Me, too," Ben laughed.

The next 60 minutes was a blur of activity, and all was going smoothly until . . . Jake reached for the eggs. One started rolling across the counter, and as he leaned forward to retrieve it, his shoe slipped on the slick kitchen floor. And then his arm knocked the egg, which sent it flying into Heather's back, where it splattered.

"Hey!" Heather screamed. She jerked her head back toward her shoulder to see gooey yoke dripping from her sweater.

"Oh my God! I'm *so* sorry!" Jake said, grabbing a wet rag to help remove the mess.

"Ugh! I was going to wear this again," Heather wailed. "It used to be my lucky sweater—can you believe it? But just look at it now," she huffed, as she tried to de-egg herself.

"Can I buy you a new one?" Jake said, scrambling to find the right words.

"Well, sure—thanks," she said, handing Jake a fresh egg and wringing out the remains of goo. "I know you didn't mean to do it."

"Thank you. I really didn't. And about yesterday, I'm sorry about ditching you so fast after the taping. That was rude."

"Don't worry about it," Heather smiled.

"Thanks for understanding. Ben and I have got a lot going on. Maybe one of these days I'll tell you about it."

Jake returned to the counter where he and Ben were working and repositioned himself so that any debris from his beating the eggs would splash the opposite way. *Geeze, somewhere over the Atlantic Ocean, I became a complete klutz. I don't get it.*

*   *   *

"Second place! I'll take it." Ben grinned as he finished wiping the counter clean after their morning bake.

"And it's nice that Heather took first. She works so hard, doing everything without a partner," Jake said. "Ready to go?" Seeing Ben nod his head, he added, "I hope Sophie was able to find the drone and the camera so we can try some remote reconnaissance."

"She's pretty smart, so I bet she did."

As they left the building, they saw a cab with a green TAXI PARISIEN sign approaching, and Ben quickly hailed it.

"That was lucky," Jake said, climbing into the back seat. Traffic was light and the taxi soon arrived at the park's edge, where they saw Sophie waiting. Beside her were three duffle bags. Jake paid the driver and hopped out.

"Good call putting all the stuff in duffle bags, Sophie," Jake said, grabbing one bag while Ben took another. "Thanks!" Having reviewed topographical and satellite imagery on the internet, Jake had identified a spot in the park that offered the most seclusion from prying eyes and was within range of the island.

"Here is good." Jake stopped and placed his duffle bag on the ground. Ben and Sophie gently placed their duffels beside his. Jake peered through the branches of the trees lining the lake and nodded in silent approval.

"*Parfait*, no sign of the guards." *Hey, I'm picking up more French*, Jake thought. *There's hope for me, after all!* He unzipped one of the duffels and pulled out a drone that spanned nearly 18 inches.

"Camera." Jake held his hand out like a surgeon waiting for a scalpel.

Ben opened a different bag and extracted a small Wi-Fi camera. "Why didn't we just buy a drone with a built-in camera?"

"That type doesn't have the range we need. It's a good 300 yards from here to inside the stone walls of the grotto." Jake used zip ties to attach the camera to the front of the copter.

Ben clambered up a nearby tree and taped a Wi-Fi range-extender to a large branch. He then ran power cables down to a battery pack that Sophie had removed from one of the bags.

"We're all set up," Ben said, as he dropped to the ground. "Just give me a sec to sync the camera to my tablet."

Jake waited patiently for Ben to run through a series of internet screens and IP configuration pages.

"Try it." Ben pointed to the camera. Jake lifted the drone and rotated it while looking at the screen. Whatever he pointed its nose toward, he could see on Ben's computer.

"Perfect, my friend. Perfect." Jake high-fived Ben.

"Very impressive. You guys are geniuses," Sophie said.

Jake grinned at her. "Thanks. More creative out of necessity than genius. Okay, time to lift off." Jake put the drone in the middle of the clearing and powered it on. Using the remote, he started the blades and slowly adjusted the altitude until the copter hovered 10 feet above them.

"How's the image?"

"There's a bit of jitter but all in all, okay," Ben replied.

Jake maneuvered the drone around the clearing, practicing his flying skills. He then stopped looking at the machine itself and tried to fly it looking solely at Ben's screen. "I don't think we can use the full automated drone mode as we don't know what's in the grotto, but this is hard. It's like driving while looking through a straw instead of a windshield."

"Maybe you should let your right brain take over?" Ben joked.

"Ha-ha. I think that only works when you're drawing," Jake said, but a moment later he was whispering to himself, "Left, up a bit, forward . . ." *Just in case it helps,* he thought.

After practicing for a few more minutes, Jake increased the drone's altitude until it could clear the large trees hugging the shore. He directed it to fly straight toward the 200-foot-long bridge that connected the island with the rest of park.

"Follow the bridge onto the island. It will lead us into the artificial cave," Sophie said. "That's what my grandmother was remembering."

The image on the screen showed a footpath. As Jake pushed forward on the joystick, the drone traveled along the walkway. The grotto had a wide entrance, which allowed enough light for the camera to work and made it easy for Jake to operate the craft.

"We're in! Whoa, this place is cool. The stone and the darkness make it look like a real cave and not some manmade creation," Ben exclaimed.

"I know! Can you believe it's right in the middle of the city? There, Jake! A little to the left," Sophie said, pointing to the water cascading down the wall inside the cave. "Bubbe said they would enjoy their snack left over from their picnic by that little recess in the wall next to the waterfall."

"You sure?"

"Yes. She said she would play games with Naomi while leaning against the smooth part of the wall."

"Ben, any sign of our friends?"

Ben, who had been sitting closer to the shore where he could scan the footbridge for activity, called back. "All clear!"

Using a grid search style, Jake maneuvered the drone in slow climbs and descents to scan every section of the interior cave wall and floor. *Hope Ben's video capture program is working. No time to check now.*

"Okay, we're done. Let's get out of here." He swiveled the helicopter around toward the exit when suddenly, a flash of blue filled the screen.

Then, everything went dark.

10

ANOTHER MYSTERY?

"What happened?" Jake jiggled the controls. "We've lost visual!"

Ben sprinted back to his tablet and rewound the video recording.

"There—stop there!" Sophie said. Ben hit "pause" and they all went silent as the blurry but recognizable image of one of the security guards appeared on the screen.

"Did we get enough video?" Ben asked.

"I think so. Let's beat it before they come out here looking for us," Jake said.

* * *

For the next hour, the three of them sat at an outdoor table of a brasserie and scrutinized the five minutes of video the drone had captured.

"People have walked around this place for 70 years since the last time Dahlia was here. I don't think we're going to see anything helpful on this tiny screen," Jake said.

"I agree," Sophie said. "We need to actually feel the stone and look for cracks and clues."

"I've been thinking, though, that the riddle says 'treasure.' I assume that means people's stuff. How could it be hidden in the grotto? I looked at pictures online and it isn't a *large* cave, is it?"

"Not really. But maybe there's an *entrance* that leads to an area below it?" Ben asked.

"Underneath! You *are* a genius!" Sophie exclaimed. "I know where we can look next, and we *won't* be trespassing in the park. Listen, after your bake-off tomorrow, meet me at an address that I'll text you, and wear clothes you don't care about . . . if you happen to have any."

The kids said goodbye and headed in opposite directions.

When the boys arrived at Aunt Jenna's apartment, they decided not to go up. "Let's walk down to the Seine for a while before dinner," Jake suggested. "We have plenty of time."

Although it wasn't high tourist season, the shops along the Seine were crowded with visitors. The scene was like a mini-melting pot, with people speaking languages from at least a dozen different countries.

"It's pretty busy here," Jake muttered.

"Yes. I'm guessing if you lived here, you would avoid this area," Ben replied.

"Like at home. I haven't been near the Empire State Building or Times Square in years."

Shimmering in the moonlight, the Seine looked exactly the way it did in the guidebooks. The monuments and bridges were beautifully illuminated, and as tour boats floated past, flashes from the passengers' cameras made the boats twinkle like the stars in the indigo sky.

"Which way should we walk?" Ben asked, as he leaned over the rail to look at the rippling water.

"We probably don't have enough time to go all the way to the Eiffel Tower, but let's head in that direction anyway for a bit." Jake turned right, enjoying the grandeur of the stately buildings. "How come this place wasn't leveled during

World War II like all the other cities?"

"I read that when the Germans approached, Paris declared itself an Open City, meaning it was undefended, so the army didn't shell it. When the Americans came to liberate it, most of the German army was gone, and those who remained weren't able to do much damage because the Resistance took over key areas," Ben said.

"I should have read up more on the history before coming here—especially since I'm related to Dahlia, who was a part of all of it." Jake scuffed a pebble with his toe.

"Don't beat yourself up. You didn't know about Dahlia before we got here."

"Kind of ironic," Jake huffed.

"What is?"

"People were led to believe that the Jews were ruining their country, so they followed Hitler, who actually ended up ruining their country."

"Hitler ruined the *world*," Ben said.

*　　*　　*

The boys got so engrossed in their discussions about the contest and the mystery they were unraveling that they passed Jenna's street and had to double back. Suddenly, Jake stopped and inclined his head slightly. "See that moped rider up there? It's the same one who was outside the police station—I know it." He nodded toward the rider without making it too obvious. "Red helmet with a black visor. And I saw him when we were leaving the baking contest before that. I remember thinking it was odd because the helmet was super new but the bike was junk."

Without any warning to Ben, Jake started running up the street. "Hey, you there!"

The rider gunned the throttle, and the moped flew off, quickly outpacing Jake.

58

"Well, it *looks* old but the engine sure works," Ben panted, catching up to Jake in the middle of the street.

"Think it's related to the guards?" Jake asked.

"Not if it's the same person who was outside the baking contest. The guards didn't know we existed until we showed up at the park," Ben answered.

"Great, *another* mystery to solve. So much for sleeping tonight," Jake said as he and Ben headed into the apartment building.

11

A REAL CHALLENGE AND BAKE 3

Jake couldn't help staring at the dish in the center of the table.

"Thank you for making breakfast, Aunt Jenna," Ben said, as he kicked Jake's foot under the table, trying to rouse him from his trance.

"Yes. It looks . . . delicious," Jake said.

"It's an experimental dish I thought I'd try for you: oatmeal-bake with veggie sausage links."

Jake stared at the rectangular pan filled with thick oatmeal and brownish sausage pieces, and at the cat-handled serving spoon beside it. *I'm eating a litter box for breakfast*, he thought.

When Ben saw Jake eyeing Romeo, who had come into the room, he kicked his friend again, as if he could read his mind.

"Aaaanyway," Ben said, trying to change the monologue in Jake's head and introduce a different topic of conversation, "today will be quite a challenge."

But probably not as hard as trying to paw through this oatmeal mixture, Jake thought.

"We'll all be working from the same recipe, so we'll have to rely on our creativity to make a standout dish. They'll be taking our phones away, too, so we'll need to prepare." Ben tried to swallow a spoonful without grimacing, eyes glued to his tablet.

"You can't cram for something if you don't know what the challenge will be, Ben. You might as well sit back and enjoy your breakfast—clear your mind," Jake said, trying not to laugh.

"I bet Sophie would be handy here. She could memorize all the baking techniques in a recipe book and be ready for anything," Ben replied.

"Could be. I don't know why, but I feel a bit envious."

"It's because you're competitive, Jake. Seeing others do better than you fuels you, like how you became first chair violin," Ben said.

"Until you came around and made me second fiddle again," Jake grinned.

"Ha-ha, not technically a pun, but I'll count it," Ben said.

"Are you saying that my music joke struck a chord?" Jake replied.

"Now *that's* what I was looking for!"

*   *   *

The bakers lined up in front of their stations and waited for Jacques to make his announcement.

"I hope this is a fast bake so we can run back to Jenna's to pick up our coats and still meet Sophie on time," Jake muttered.

"Today's challenge is a three-layered torte. It will be composed of 20 ingredients and will require 22 steps to bake. Read the recipe thoroughly and have your tempting torte ready in three hours," he recited. "And contestants, let's *bake* the world a *batter* place than when we came in today, shall we?" With that, he departed to a chorus of groans.

Jake watched as Heather started to put two aprons on, one in front and one in back.

"Just to be safe," she said playfully.

"Very funny," Jake replied.

"I'll handle the sponge and you tackle the pastry cream, okay?" Ben suggested.

"Yep." Jake poured the milk, sugar, salt, and vanilla bean seeds into a saucepan and turned up the gas burner to medium heat. He glanced to his right as Ben combined the two flours and the salt.

When the sponge cake layers were cooling on the wire racks and the pastry cream was chilling in the fridge, Ben called to Jake, "Let's roll out the marzipan!"

"On it!" Jake pushed back their mountain of dishes to create space, cleaned the surface, and spread powdered sugar over it to ensure that the marzipan wouldn't stick. He was mindful not to throw the sugar too hard, lest it get on Heather, who was standing just a few feet away. *How does she do it without any help?* Jake thought, as he watched her move her own marzipan to the table.

"Ready!" Jake stepped back as Ben kneaded the marzipan into a ball.

"Reminds me of your dough in Chicago," Jake said.

"Let's hope not—that dough was so sticky!" Ben replied. "If this gets sticky, we'll just add more sugar." Ben pushed down on the marzipan with a rolling pin to flatten it into a disk—large enough to cover the cake. After a minute or two, he said, "Here, Jake, why don't you roll it out the rest of the way. I shouldn't have all the fun! You can stop when it's a quarter-inch thick."

"Thanks!" Jake took the rolling pin from Ben, but just as he was about to step into position, he slipped on some spilled milk. With the rolling pin still in his hand, he tried to keep from falling by reaching forward and slamming it onto the counter. Jake watched in horror as the rolling pin struck a jam-filled spoon, which catapulted into the air.

Ugh. He knew exactly where it would land.

"Argh!" Heather screamed. She turned and glared at Jake, raspberry jam dripping from her face and blouse. "Are you *trying* to sabotage me, Jake?"

"No, of course not! Oh my God, I am *so, so* sorry, Heather! It was an accident. They've *all* been accidents." Jake offered a clean rag to her as he apologized over and over again. She took the rag, shot him a look of irritation, and then turned back to her station to finish her torte.

"Dude, they got that on *camera*," Ben laughed. "I bet they show the flying spoon in slow motion when this airs on TV. It'll be *epic*."

"Thanks, pal," Jake murmured. *He's right, of course. Up next: The klutz in the kitchen strikes again! I hope Heather believes I'm not trying to hurt her chances,* Jake thought. Ben finished rolling out the marzipan while Jake worked on the chocolate ganache that would adorn their dessert.

Ding!

"Time's up! We can't wait to *feast* our eyes on your master-pieces!" Jacques called out. "But of course, as the saying goes, the proof of the pudding is in the eating. Judges, are you ready?"

Jake and Ben stood back, waiting for them to make their rounds. Jake's stomach tightened with anticipation and nervousness. *I want to win this contest for Ben. He'll surely be able to get into any cooking school he wants if we win.*

In the end, the team from India received the third day's top spot. Jake and Ben took second place, slightly edging out Heather, who received a deduction because her sponge layers were a little uneven. The teens from Sweden were eliminated from the competition.

"Sorry again about the spoon. I don't know how this keeps happening to me . . . er, to you," Jake said. "You know what I mean. I'm not *normally* so clumsy," he assured her as they waited to receive their instructions for the next day's bake. "I really don't know what's wrong with me."

"It's okay—really, no worries. I just snapped because I

knew I wasn't going to finish on top. I can do better than third. Just try to be more careful tomorrow," Heather replied. "Besides, my father always says, 'If you don't want to get messy, get out of the kitchen.'"

"Seems like a good rule for life in general," Jake replied, laughing. "Your dad sounds pretty smart."

Heather's face softened. "He is. Smart *and* the hardest worker I've ever seen. We didn't have much money when I was younger. He worked two jobs so he could pay for baking school to follow his dream while also ensuring we never went hungry and always had presents for birthdays and under the tree each Christmas."

"Wow! He must be pretty happy to see you here, following in his footsteps," Jake said.

"Actually, he doesn't know I'm here. Because it's so hard to make a living in the kitchen, he wants a different life for me. But I'm a baker—I feel it in my—"

"Spatulas?" Ben interjected. "Get it?"

"Good one!" Jake reached up for a high-five.

"Yes, spatulas—scapulas. I get it," she responded, smiling. "You're quick! Anyway, I feel it in my *bones.* I want to win to show my dad that I *can* succeed so he won't keep pushing me into a field I don't have the heart for. I told him and my mom that I was coming to Paris on a school field trip."

The judges returned, and Meredith gave out the details for the fourth day's bake. "You must bake something French. It can be anything you want, but it must have its origins in France. So go out tonight, experience this beautiful city, and channel your inner Parisian."

"In other words, have a *beret* good time!" Jacques added with a wink.

"How could we not?" said Ben. "Paris is a *Seine*-sational city!"

"Awesome!" Jake laughed. "Can I use that line for one of the captions to my drawings?"

"*Naturellement!*" Ben said.

12

CATAPHILES

"Stop here!" Jake pointed, signaling for the driver to pull over. He and Ben hopped out and joined Sophie, who was dressed in dark clothing. Beside her on the sidewalk stood another teenage girl. Jake pegged her as a high school junior or maybe even a senior. Her jeans and shirt were stained and torn, and her backpack was faded and fraying. She was chewing a large wad of gum.

Not exactly the picture of Parisian style. "I'm Jake." He extended a hand.

"No names, *s'il vous plaît.* New people tend to get caught and I don't want you turning me in." The girl's English wasn't as polished as Sophie's, and her thick French accent seemed to lend a clandestine aura to their meeting. "We are going into the Catacombs, into a section that is not very popular. No good party spots," she continued, as she walked them toward the entrance of an apartment building.

"Cataphile? You're a cataphile?" Ben asked.

"Translate?" Jake muttered.

"The Catacombs are a big web of tunnels that hold the bones of people who died centuries ago—there are even walls and objects made of skulls and bones. There are guided tours of the public areas, but most of the tunnels are off-limits, so cataphiles are people who ignore the rules and explore the restricted areas," Ben explained.

"Oh, *now* the no-name thing makes sense. How did you find this entrance?" Jake asked.

"You don't need to know. By the way, you two aren't exactly dressed for this." She looked at Jake's and Ben's new-looking pants and shoes.

"They didn't have time to scuff themselves up," Sophie interjected.

"Too late to worry about that now," she mumbled to herself. The girl knocked on a side door of one of the small basement apartments. A woman answered. Instant recognition registered on her face when she saw their guide.

"Pay her. Twenty euros," the girl instructed.

Jake quickly peeled off a bill from the small roll of money he was carrying.

The woman opened the door all the way and escorted them back to a small bedroom. She pushed aside an antique three-drawer dresser to reveal a small metal door—*big enough for a good-sized Labrador retriever to fit through,* Jake thought, *but a very tight squeeze for us humans.*

As the cataphile pulled flashlights from her bag and handed them out, Sophie whispered to Jake, "This apartment once belonged to the woman's grandparents, who fought in the Resistance. They used the caves to transport contraband, to hide in after sabotage missions, and to shelter Jews and others during mass arrests. Her wall bordered a tunnel, so they created a pathway."

"Thank you, Sophie," Jake said quietly. "By the way, how do you know our guide?"

Sophie shook her head to say "not now," as the owner motioned for them to duck down and crawl in. The cataphile casually popped a small bubble she'd formed with her gum and said, "Wait—not yet. Before you enter, please leave your phones, wallets, and any other identification here."

"Why?" Ben asked.

"It's the way of the Resistance. No markings or ways they can identify you if you're caught."

"But we're not in the Resis—"

A stern look from Sophie cut Jake off and he quickly complied with the demand.

The air in the tunnels was just as Jake expected: thick and clammy. Although there were only a few puddles, the ground was moist with scattered stones, and Jake could feel the mud caking on his shoes.

The tunnel soon branched out in several directions. The girl referred to her notebook, chose one of the paths, and then chose again and again at every intersection.

With each bend and turn in the tunnel, Jake became more nervous. *Ben was right about a web of tunnels. But it's okay to not be in charge; just follow and trust her,* Jake reminded himself. *We won't get lost. We won't get lost.*

As if reading his mind, the cataphile began to act as a tour guide, sharing interesting information as they walked. "Here is a little-known fact: This watertight passageway under the lake was created by the same engineer and architect who created the Eiffel Tower *and* the 63-meter suspension bridge that connects to the island where the grotto is located."

"And," Ben added, "Gustave Eiffel also designed the iron armature for the Statue of Liberty—"

"Which," Sophie interjected, "was a gift from France to the American people!"

"*D'accord*, we just finished passing under the lake, so these next 20 meters will be in line with where you think this hidden chamber might be." The guide indicated a stretch of wall. "I suggest you look closely at the wall to see if you notice disturbances that suggest another tunnel. We find them from time to time. Dirt that was moved 60 years ago looks different from the original tunnel wall."

"How do you know we're near the grotto and have passed under the lake?" Jake couldn't help himself. It's not that he didn't trust her, but as his dad liked to say, "Trust but verify."

"The main reason is that it's cooler here than where we entered. There are other reasons, of course, but we don't have time to go into those now. Besides, one day, I'm going to write a book about the tunnels down here . . . maybe a doctoral paper."

Jake, Ben, and Sophie spread out along the wall, looking for the slightest changes in the dirt. But each time one of them thought they'd found something, their guide would quickly assess it and pronounce it as natural or not a potential secondary chamber below the park's grotto.

After about 30 minutes of searching, Jake was discouraged. "We should probably give up. Doesn't appear to be anything here."

The others, exhausted and cold, agreed. But just as the group crossed back under the lake, the girl whisper-yelled, "Quiet! Turn off your lights!"

The sudden blackness and deafening silence were overwhelming. After a few seconds, Jake could hear the patter of steps and saw a faint glow of light coming their way. In that instant, Jake felt transported in time, as if he were a French Jew hiding out from the Nazis. The boot steps grew louder.

"Follow me!" their guide said in a hushed but urgent tone. She turned on a special dim-red flashlight and started running.

Despite her caution, an approaching voice called out, "*Arrêtez, arrêtez—la police!*" The police switched their flashlights to high beam and their footsteps turned to a run. The kids turned on their white lights and sprinted. Jake was the farthest back and therefore the closest to danger. He ran as fast as he could after the disappearing forms of his friends. As he skittered around a corner, he slipped on the muddy surface of the tunnel floor and found himself flat on the ground. He scooped up his flashlight and returned to his feet just in time to feel strong hands gripping his collar. A bright light shone in his face as he felt the cold steel of handcuffs snapping around his wrists.

13

MILLENNIUM FALCON

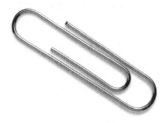

The policemen spoke in rapid French as they hauled Jake down the tunnel.

"Are we going to the station in the 19th *arrondissement?*" Jake asked.

"No, we are not," one of them said in gruff English.

Uh-oh, Chevy may not be able to help me then—I need to figure a way out of this! One of the policemen led the way with his flashlight, while the other held Jake by the elbow and walked shoulder to shoulder with him. The narrow pathways made the going slow. *Good . . . I need time to think!*

The cuffs were tight, but Jake could still feel the telltale hole pattern of the Smith and Wesson Model 100 hand-cuffs, a worldwide favorite of law enforcement. He'd become familiar with this model through his job with the home security shop back in New York. Recognizing the cuffs gave him a surge of confidence. Though his hands were cuffed behind him and the officer had a firm grip on his elbow, he was still able to reach into his back pocket where he had stuffed a Paris Métro map. He'd paper clipped a few notes to the map for easy reference. The police had searched him for identification, weapons, and cell phones but had left the paper in his pocket. He was thankful for the cataphile's paranoia in making him leave his ID at the apartment. *If I can get away, they won't know who I am or where to look!*

It was the paper clip he was after, not the papers. His hands were muddy from searching the wall for clues, and he had to concentrate on walking carefully in the tunnel and being discrete about his movements, but slowly and carefully Jake straightened the clip. He thought about the times he'd spent practicing escaping from handcuffs during breaks at the security shop back home. *It sure was a lot easier in that warm and well-lit building.* He slid the thin wire into the lock hole, bent it 90 degrees one direction, and then turned the wire and made another slight bend in the makeshift key. Then he gently threaded the wire into the handcuff mechanism, feeling for the slight lip inside the lock.

Nothing. *Patience, Jake.*

Jake tried to picture the lock in his head. Again, he slid the wire into the locking mechanism. Once he was sure he was past the lip, he pressed upward with a firm and consistent pressure. As the lock began to give, Jake coughed loudly to cover up the clicking sound. The policemen plodded on, signifying they hadn't heard the steel bracelets loosening. Using his fingers, Jake held the cuffs in place so it would appear as if they were still locked around his wrists.

They came to a staircase with tall risers. Jake struggled to climb with his hands behind his back. At the top of the stairs, a large metal door blocked the way. The policeman in the lead pulled a key from his pocket to unlock it. Jake squinted as the bright light of day hit him in the face and found himself being hustled between the two officers down a moderately busy sidewalk. Passersby stared at him, no doubt wondering about his offense. As they approached a street corner, Jake saw an empty patrol car waiting by the curb. One officer dropped Jake's arm and reached into his pocket for keys.

Now or never! Jake took a deep breath, turned his head to the officer still holding his other arm, and screamed at the top of his lungs.

"I'm sorry!"

His shout had the desired effect. Startled by the sudden sound, the policeman momentarily loosened his grip, allowing Jake to rip his arm free. Bolting to his right, he sprinted down the sidewalk, zigzagging his way around the surprised pedestrians.

God, I hope I'm losing them! The handcuff was still attached to his left wrist and with each stride, it swung violently into his elbow. He ignored the pain as he poured on the speed. Up ahead, he saw the art deco Métro sign beckoning him. He hopped onto the handrail—the damp mud on his pants acting like a lubricant—and slid at surprising speed toward the bottom of the stairs. He heard shouts behind him and assumed the policemen were pushing their way through the people climbing up.

Tumbling off the rail, Jake scrambled to his feet. Risking a quick glance, he spotted the policemen a dozen yards behind him.

Jake ran toward the ticket booth, jumped the turnstiles, and continued into the bowels of the train station. He dodged a large group of tourists studying a map and headed toward the sound of a train slowing down. He was on an elevated platform and could see the train arriving below him. He turned toward the stairs, momentarily forgetting about the two men pursuing him and focusing instead on his escape route. The train's doors opened as he bounded down the stairs toward them. *One-thousand, two-thousand, three-thousand.* During yesterday's trip, he had inexplicably timed the duration of the open doors—it was just something his mind did automatically—so he knew they would stay in that position for 20 seconds.

His mental clock was at 15 seconds when he reached the bottom of the staircase and found himself on a wide platform. *The doors are about to close!* He made a dash for it. And like the Millennium Falcon navigating the inner guts of the Death Star, Jake turned himself sideways to avoid getting snagged and slipped between the doors just as they slammed shut. He felt himself tumble into a passenger and glanced up in time to see the policemen running alongside the car, shouting into their radios.

14

YOU GOTTA HAVE FRIENDS

"You've got to be kidding me! Again?" a familiar voice called from above.

Jake clambered to his feet and stared in surprise. "Heather! Oh, God, I'm so sorry!" he wheezed. He had rammed right into her, smearing mud all over her clothes. *What are the odds?!*

"And I just finished shopping for new clothes." She pointed to the bags at her feet.

"I know, I know. I will pay for *all* of your clothes, I promise, but right now, you have to help me. Please. I'm in trouble," Jake stammered.

"Those cops were chasing *you?*" Heather's eyes dropped to the handcuff still dangling from Jake's wrist.

"Yes." Jake shoved his hand into his pocket to hide the handcuff from the other passengers. He gave her a rapid-fire version of the story about Esther, Sophie, and Dahlia. Some nearby passengers leaned in to listen.

"So you want to find this book to reunite people with their long-lost treasures?" Heather asked.

"Yes. I know it sounds crazy, but could I really make up a story that fast? I need to find that book and find out who *I am* in the process. I always thought I knew where my family was from, but now I realize I've only known half of it," Jake replied.

"We need to hide you, then." Heather motioned to the nearby passengers to gather around. She pulled a long dress out of her bag and handed it to Jake.

"Here, put this on," she said. She donned a new sweater herself, covering the mud that Jake had smeared on her.

"Take my hat, too, young man." An older woman removed her wide-brimmed, floppy hat and offered it to Jake.

"We'll form a circle around you when we exit," Heather said, enlisting willing strangers to form a visual barrier around Jake.

Finally! Being short pays off, Jake thought, as he realized everyone else around him was at least a head taller. Heather tucked Jake's muddy backpack into the bottom of one of her shopping bags.

As he expected, Paris's *gendarmes* were flooding the next Métro platform. *Seems a bit like overkill for a trespasser,* Jake thought, shielding his face with the hat.

"Skip the escalators—it will make us too visible. Aim for that elevator," Heather instructed. Like a plump of geese, the group pivoted as one and wedged themselves into the elevator.

"I can't express how much I appreciate this," Jake said, after the doors closed behind them.

"Well, it's not every day we get to be involved in a good cause," said the woman who'd donated her hat. The others voiced their agreement, nodding and patting Jake on the back.

Moments later, they exited onto the main floor. With Heather calling out commands, the group left the station, and Jake quietly thanked the helpful strangers.

"I got us a car," Heather said, as a sedan with a ride-share placard pulled up to the curb. "Now take me to Sophie, Jake. I want to help."

Ben, Sophie, and their guide were standing in front of the apartment building where they had entered the Catacombs. The relief on their faces was visible when they realized it was Jake getting out of the car, though Ben laughed until tears formed in his eyes at the sight of Jake in a dress.

Jake introduced Heather and gave a quick recap of his escape.

"You picked the handcuffs?" the guide asked, her voice filled with disbelief.

Jake held up his wrists, the cuffs dangling from only one. Using the paper clip, he popped off the other cuff in a matter of seconds. "I would have removed it earlier, but I thought if I had popped it off easily in front of the others on the Métro, that might have made me look *really* suspicious."

"Good thinking. My name is Claire, by the way." She offered Jake her hand—as well as his wallet and cell phone.

"Jake. Very pleased to officially meet you. Now I think I should get out of these clothes and back to a safer area before someone spots us." Jake motioned for the others to enter the car still waiting by the curb.

Before they had arrived back at Aunt Jenna's, Sophie's cell phone chimed.

"It's Chevy." She put it on speaker. "We're all here," she said.

"Good. I heard about some young people escaping police officers in the restricted area of the Catacombs near the park. I'm sure you don't know anything about that."

Jake's blood pressure spiked until he realized that Chevy wasn't waiting for an answer. He already knew, and he wasn't about to turn them in.

"I have a possible lead. Can you meet me in front of the National Archives at 2:00 tomorrow?"

"Yes, sure," everyone answered in unison.

"Good. One more thing. I need you all to wear matching blue shirts."

15

CLOTHES MAKE THE MAN

Safely back at Aunt Jenna's apartment, Jake tucked the hand-cuffs into his suitcase, changed into clean clothes, and then headed out with Ben, Sophie, Claire, and Heather to shop for matching blue shirts.

Interested in helping Sophie and impressed with Jake's ingenuity, Claire had decided to join their cause. "After we find the shirts, I think you two, Jake and Ben, should try to look more European by changing your shoes and those American-looking jeans," she suggested.

"Thanks! Makes sense. If Chevy wants us to look alike, we can't make it seem obvious that we're American," Jake said. He remembered with chagrin how the police officer at the reception desk had known instantly where they were from.

Finding the shirts was easy. Picking out pants and shoes took more time. To break them in so they wouldn't look brand-new, they wore them out of the store and headed for the Eiffel Tower. At the Trocadéro Gardens, the boys trotted up and down the steps overlooking the Warsaw Fountain, scuffing the shoes a bit and wearing some of the sheen off their stylish corduroy pants. The girls watched and smiled from the low wall of the terrace, where they were sitting and enjoying some chocolate crêpes and the singular view of the wrought-iron lattice tower.

"Five more times, just to be safe," Claire teased, when the boys returned sweaty and worn out.

"Ha-ha," Jake grinned.

Jake and Ben dug into their own crêpes as they watched the boats motor past on the river.

"Just a heads-up. We think someone is following Jake and me, so keep your eye out for a white moped with a rider in a red helmet," Ben warned.

"When did this start?" Heather asked.

"We think from one of the first days we were here. Not sure," Jake replied with a mouthful of chocolate.

"I wonder what that's all about," Claire said.

16

OOPS AND BAKE 4

Jake was still wondering about the moped when he woke up at 7:00 the next morning. He and Ben barely had time to eat breakfast before heading to the baking contest, where Jacques, as high-spirited as ever, shared the instructions for that morning's bake, set the clock for three hours, and told the contestants: "We can't wait to see your confection collection!"

"Now he's rhyming," Ben snickered. Jake and Ben crisscrossed the kitchen, grabbing ingredients. Before bed, they'd made a mock-up of the contest's kitchen and used the little green army men Jake kept in his backpack to rehearse their movements. ROC drills, as his great-uncle called them—drills for rehearsal of concept. He'd served in the prestigious Irish Defense Force Rangers, and Jake tried to absorb his knowledge every time they talked.

Like a precision NASCAR pit crew, Jake and Ben handed each other ingredients and tools without a word. Within minutes, the brioche dough was ready to go into the proofing oven to rise, first for 90 minutes and then again for 30 minutes.

Jake paused before removing the dough from the oven to watch Heather, who was smoothly alternating between caramelizing sliced almonds on the stove and rotating baking trays of meringue in the oven. *She's a real baker.*

"Earth to Jake. Time to make the pastry cream!" Ben's voice roused Jake, who took that as his cue to remove the dough from the oven.

Jake returned to their rehearsed plan and helped Ben gather the ingredients for the custard filling. While Ben heated the vanilla beans, milk, egg yolks, flour, cornstarch, and orange blossom water, Jake started to melt the dark chocolate for the decorations. They had discovered some Eiffel Tower molds in the contest's well-stocked equipment room and decided to place a few chocolate towers atop the bread. Soon enough, the bread was in the oven, baking at 180 degrees Celsius for 30 minutes, and the now-cooled cream was ready to be whipped with icing sugar.

I wonder if Gustave knew how symbolic his tower would become, Jake thought, waiting for the chocolate to harden in the molds. *What a feat for an architect, to create something so recognizable and treasured.* Famous pictures of the Eiffel Tower flooded his mind, interrupted each time by the picture of Hitler standing in front of it. *What a tragedy: fear and hatred of a group of people led to unimaginable atrocities. What would I have done if I had been there? Would I have been heroic like Dahlia?*

"Jake, the brioche!" Ben yelled. He had taken a quick bathroom break and now came running back to the kitchen, despondent at the sound of the timer's insistent beep. Jake snapped into the present, yanking the bread out of the oven.

"Sorry!" he said, as he fanned the bread with his hand in a useless gesture to cool it.

"We've only got 20 minutes left. Slice it on the plate so it will cool faster, and then I'll add the cream."

Using a few paper towels as insulation, Jake held the bread with one hand and sliced it horizontally. He tried hard to ignore the intrusive cameraman, who was filming close-ups of their moment of crisis.

"Brioche isn't supposed to crackle when you cut into it, is it?" Jake felt his shoulders droop.

"No-o-o-o," Ben moaned.

I've let my buddy down. Daydreaming again—what's wrong with me?! Jake threw the baking sheet into the sink.

SPLASH! It caught the handle of a measuring cup that was soaking, sending a spray of water across the room. Jake's stomach tightened as he calculated the trajectory.

Heather didn't say a word as the water landed on her back, soaking her light silk blouse. Her eyes, part death-glare and part disappointment, said it all.

Now I've let her down too, Jake thought.

"Time!" Jacques called, just as Ben placed the top half of the brioche over the filling and Jake placed the chocolate towers on top. Silently, the teams stepped away from their creations.

Jake didn't feel nervous as the judges made their way through the entries. *I know we failed. And it's all my fault. I'll have to make this up to Ben. But how?*

Ben elbowed Jake gently. "Don't worry—it's just one part of the contest."

Jake swallowed hard. "Am I that easy to read?"

"Being the best isn't as important as being content. We're in Paris, we've made some new friends, we're solving a major mystery, and we're eating pastry fit for a king!"

A warmth grew inside Jake—it was great to have a friend who saw things the way Ben did. "True. Always helps to know how fortunate we really are."

François and Meredith stopped in front of the boys' dish. They each cut a slice and tasted it.

"*La Tarte Tropézienne* is a tough bake. Kudos on having the courage to try it. Although the flavors are good and the aroma is divine—vanilla with orange blossom is my favorite—the separation inside the bread tells me it was over-proofed,"

Meredith said, as she set her plate down.

"Over-proofed and overbaked. It feels as though I'm chewing sand." François dropped his plate on the table, sending a loud clatter through the otherwise quiet kitchen.

Jake felt Heather's hand briefly rest on his shoulder before the judges turned their attention to her creation.

"*La Dacquoise*, a sweet meringue and cream bisquit," Meredith said.

"What flavors have you used?" François asked.

"It's a hazelnut coffee cream layered with caramelized almonds in between the meringue," Heather replied.

"Exquisite," François commented as he took a bite.

"Indeed. The meringue is light and airy, just as it should be, and the cream is rich, but not overpowering. Delicious. Marvelous work," Meredith added.

Everyone clapped as Heather was announced the winner of that day's competition.

"Congratulations, Heather," Jake said. "Well-deserved." He gave her a quick hug.

"Thank you. I can't believe the French team burned their dish," she replied.

"Ironic that they exit on the day Jake and I bake something French. I think because we tried something special, that gave us a little bit of an edge. Otherwise, we might have been toast," Ben chuckled.

"I agree, although François probably thinks our brioche *was* toast!" Jake couldn't resist joking. "Okay, are we all ready to head to the Archives?" he asked.

Heather nodded and the three of them headed out of the building.

"So we have one last bake before the finale. This is where I really get stressed. I don't want to go out right before the final round. I'd rather go out on Day One than get this close to the finale and *then* lose," Ben said.

"I'm sure you guys will make it. It's down to you, me, the Norwegians, and the Dutch team," Heather said.

"Yes, but it's a mystery bake, so we won't be able to practice, which means—"

"Moped at nine o'clock!" Ben interrupted.

Jake's eyes darted to the left and he spotted the moped and rider. "Heather, that's the guy we were talking about. Let's turn right and walk through that little park we saw before. There's a Métro stop on the other side that's an interchange. He won't know what line we're picking up."

"Got it. And let's run to see if he's really following us." Ben jumped the last two stairs and veered right as he sprinted down the sidewalk.

Jake and Heather followed close behind, and as expected, they heard the whine of the moped as the rider gave chase. Ben's head moved back and forth as they approached the intersection.

"It's clear—run across," Ben yelled, darting toward a cluster of bushes and small trees in the park.

Jake and Heather caught up to Ben before they reached the Métro station. They stopped and looked up and down the street.

"No sign of him," Jake said as the three descended the stairs.

"We need to tell Chevy about this," Ben suggested.

"Yes," Jake said. "And I've got another idea, as well."

17

DECOY!

"*Bon, bon.* Excellent." Chevy greeted them at the entrance to the National Archives. "And whom do we have here?"

Jake, distracted by the building itself, quickly introduced Chevy to the two new members of the group, Claire and Heather. *How could anyone ever tire of this?* he wondered as his eyes darted from the tall stone pillars, steep-pitched roof, and half-dozen ornamental statues that adorned the Archive's facade.

"I'm sure you're questioning why you're here and looking alike, yes?" Chevy was dressed in his best suit. He held a clipboard and a three-ring binder with École Bilingue de Montmartre written on the side. "Well, the answer is quite simple. First, a bit of history: I told you my grandfather was a police officer during the Occupation. He lost his job and nearly his life when he went against the wishes of his superiors. He was never able to put the events of the war behind him. I was very close to him, and in his last few years, he told me how proud he was to serve the city before the war but upset that he couldn't help those being persecuted by both the Nazis *and* so many of his colleagues."

"He sounds like a good man," Heather said.

"*Merci*, he was—the best."

"So why are we at the Archives? What's the connection?" Claire asked.

"Well, I remember my grandfather telling me stories about the files they kept on local citizens. I was thinking that there might be some references to Dahlia in the records here. But unfortunately, the government does not want any further bad publicity, even now, some 70 years later. So we must, how do you say, *sneak in*," Chevy replied.

"I get it. We're a school group and you're our teacher," Jake said, pointing at Chevy's binder.

"Exactly. I need you to create a commotion while I enter the secure section and look for the files."

"Your police badge alone can't help here?" Sophie asked.

"Correct. Now gather round. I have some ideas on how you can distract the staff . . ."

"Leave that to Ben and me," Jake interrupted. "That's our area of expertise."

"*Ah, bon, your spécialité de la maison, non?*" Chevy laughed.

"Exactly!" Jake said. "Plus, we don't read French, so you, Sophie, and Claire should do the snooping. Six eyes are better than two, right?"

"What about me, Chevy?" Heather asked.

"You join us and take pictures with your phone of the documents we find linking Dahlia to the Resistance, so we can more closely look at them later."

"I can do that," Heather replied.

"*D'accord.* OK, I will lead us through the main public area and then off to the right. There is a restricted area not shown on the map that I learned may have documents from the Occupation. When I give the signal, you two boys create the distraction, and the girls and I will head to the locked record room." Chevy motioned for them to follow him.

The interior of the building was a mash-up of modern and old-fashioned decor: flat-screen televisions lined the tapestry-adorned wood-paneled walls. The modern lighting beamed down onto the marble floor. There were several tables with desktop computers. Because of the open floor plan, Jake could see rows and rows of bookshelves on the main floor as well as up on a balcony above them.

Chevy spoke rapid French to the woman behind the counter. She motioned for them to enter.

After they stepped inside, Chevy made a show of pulling his notes from the binder. "This is the French Central State section. There are 52 kilometers of material here, spanning the years 1790 to 1958. In the Archives, a volume is measured in length of shelving versus pages or numbers of documents."

"Impressive," Jake said.

"We are looking for documents pertaining to the construction of the Eiffel Tower. So if you will do as I instructed and use the guides to locate the material, we should be able to complete our search before lunch." Chevy motioned with his eyes toward the end of the room. A sign on a large oak door read *Limité*, and a guard sat in a chair beside it. By the looks of the chair and the guard, Jake could tell they'd spent a lot of time together.

"Now go to it. I'll be over there." Chevy motioned to a small table near the guard's post.

With a few bullies in their high school to contend with, Jake and Ben had often created commotions in the cafeteria or the hallways to distract them so that the victims could escape unscathed. In order to jump into action quickly, they had even begun naming some of their escapades after their favorite composers.

"Should we work up a Tchaikovsky?" Ben whispered.

"No. Too many fragile things here that we wouldn't want

to damage. I was thinking William Tell Overture," Jake replied, his eyes fixed on the guard.

Ben grinned and looked around the floor space and large wide aisles. "That oughta work just fine."

*   *   *

"Bada-dum, bada-dum, bada dum, dum, dum!" Jake straddled the chair backward and acted as if it were a horse. He trumpeted the Lone Ranger tune as Ben pushed the chair from behind. The wooden feet of the chair slid smoothly across the glossy marble floor.

"Faster, Tonto," Jake cried, as Ben pushed him down one of the aisles.

"*Arrêtez!* Stop!" the guard called out.

Ben pushed Jake and the chair into the middle of the room. The guard came striding toward them.

"Looks like bandits, Ranger. Better head for higher ground." Ben pushed the chair away from the secure room and toward a large spiral staircase that led to a balcony. The guard sped up, but not quite to a run.

Jake hopped off the chair, and he and Ben dragged it up the staircase. About halfway there, they left it on its side, blocking the pathway.

"Stop, I said!" The guard pointed at the kids.

The boys continued up onto the balcony. Jake caught a glimpse of Chevy jimmying the lock to the secure room. It opened—and he and the girls disappeared inside.

"We'll make our stand there, Tonto." Jake pointed to a small room with a glass door at the end of the balcony.

The boys sprinted into a room outfitted with computers and an ancient microfiche machine, easily outpacing the heavyset guard. Jake shut the door and Ben pushed a table in front of it, blocking the way. The guard arrived, out of breath, and tried to push his way in.

"Open up—I demand it!" he called with a thick French accent.

"*Non capisco. Sono Italiano,*" Jake replied, using the little Italian he'd been able to pick up from his friend Julie.

"You are American. I know it!" the guard replied.

"*Vorrei gli spaghetti e polpette,*" Jake replied.

Ben raised an eyebrow. "I'd like spaghetti and meatballs?" But Jake just shrugged.

A second guard showed up to join the first. This one looked more serious and intimidating and wore an "I mean business" scowl on his face.

"Things are about to get Western," Ben whispered.

"*Vorrei gli spaghetti e polpette,*" Jake repeated.

"*Tu non sei Italiano,*" the second guard said in Italian.

"Okay, we're American. And we demand to see our ambassador," Jake said.

"You will see the inside of a jail cell first if you don't come out of there," the new guard said.

Jake turned to Ben. "What do you think?"

"I think he's bluffing. No way they call the police for us locking ourselves in here for a few minutes. I don't think Chevy and the girls have had enough time. We'll open the door shortly."

Jake turned to the guards. "We'll come out in a minute. We just want to use those." Jake pointed at the microfiche machines.

"You are being ridiculous," the new guard said. He and his colleague crossed their arms and stared at the boys through the glass.

Jake bit his bottom lip and thought about Dahlia and the others who found courage to stand up to the Nazis. He pulled up a chair and sat down with his back to the guards in a show of defiance. Ben grinned and sat next to him.

Fifteen minutes later, they heard more footsteps. Two uniformed policemen appeared at the door and motioned for Jake and Ben to come out.

"Ugh, I didn't think they would call the police. We didn't damage anything. But we should give up now. If they break the door, we'll really be in for it," Jake said.

Ben nodded and slid the table away from the door. Jake stepped out, his hands in the air. To Jake's surprise, the nearest officer spun him around and for the second time in 24 hours, silver bracelets were snapped onto Jake's wrists. *I am definitely not liking this trend.*

The other officer put cuffs on Ben, who shook with distress as the officer pushed him toward the exit.

"Chevy will figure out something, buddy. Hang in there," Jake whispered with a tinge of false courage.

The guards and the policemen spoke quickly to one another in French as they walked toward the door. As they passed the secure room, Jake told himself not to look. *Don't want them to realize the others are gone.*

A police car waited by the curb, and Jake and Ben were shoved unceremoniously into the back seat. The guards and the police officers shook hands, and the police climbed into the car. There was a sick feeling in Jake's stomach that grew worse as he watched the Archives building disappear. The car was quiet as they drove through the city. Jake tried to suppress his fear. *The worst that can happen to us is that we will get sent home. Think of the Jews and the members of the Resistance during the war. Their safety and future were not as certain as ours,* Jake thought.

The police car pulled to a stop in front of a small park. Two benches sat empty under a group of linden trees blossoming in the warming spring temperatures.

The men stepped out, opened the back doors, and motioned for Jake and Ben to exit the car. The pressure on

Jake's wrists eased as one of the policemen removed his handcuffs. Ben and Jake stared at each other, then at the officers as they climbed back into the car.

"Tell Chevy he owes us," one of them said. Then the car sped off.

"Wow, what if the police had really been on the level, Jake? We took an awful risk back there."

"I know. Now that you mention it, that was *really* crazy! But if not now, when?"

"And if not us, who?" Ben asked.

"Right! We've already made a lot of connections with people and places and—and . . ."

"And family. I get it, Jake. You don't have to say any more."

18

TEA FOR SIX, S'IL VOUS PLAÎT

"Chevy is one daring planner," Jake said. Before Ben could reply, a burgundy Peugeot pulled up to the curb. Chevy was driving, with Sophie up front and Claire and Heather in the back. Claire threw the door open. Not needing any prodding, Jake and Ben stuffed themselves into the back seat.

"Thanks, Chevy! But you could have mentioned you'd lined up some help," Jake said, wiping sweat from his brow.

"*Je suis désolé*, but I wanted you to look genuinely concerned to, how do you say, *pull off* the charade?"

"Hmm, I guess it would've looked pretty bad if we'd been relaxed while being hauled away," Jake said.

"*Exactement*," he replied.

Their destination was only a few blocks away from the park: a 24-hour office supply and printing store.

"We were successful! At least I think so," Sophie said. "There were some documents that mentioned Dahlia and quite a few that discussed Jewish property."

Once inside the store, Jake followed Heather to the printing kiosk. Moments after plugging her smart phone into the cord dangling from the machine, a nearby printer whirred as grainy image after grainy image printed.

"The light wasn't the best, but we think taking pictures of

the documents worked well enough to be able to read them," Chevy explained.

"Very James Bond-ish," Ben said, nodding in approval.

Fifteen minutes and 200 pages later, the group was back in the car.

"Wish I could read French," Jake lamented.

"Well, there are also about 50 pages in German. Maybe you, Ben, and Heather can use an online translator to interpret those. It doesn't need to be an exact translation—just close enough to help us locate a clue."

"We're on it!" the three of them said in unison.

They did the work at a nearby brasserie, where they occupied a large table in the back corner and drank copious amounts of tea as they plowed through the pages. Every so often, one of them would gasp, stopping the hearts of the others; but the passages in question, though appalling or heartbreaking, were ultimately of no value to their current mission of locating the blue book and the hidden heirlooms.

"How can you drink tea while chewing gum?" Jake asked after he saw Claire refresh her gum in between pots of tea.

"I don't know. I never thought about it," Claire responded. "Of course, now that you've pointed this out, I'll probably not be able to do it again," she murmured, smiling.

"Not to pick on you, but what's with the gum, anyway? I thought the French considered it rude," Ben said.

"True, many believe it is a rude habit. We French never knew what gum was until World War II. The Americans who liberated the villages gave gum to the youngsters—my grandfather was one of them. He often told the story about how gum was his first sweet treat after the Germans were pushed out of his village. Every time I saw him, he'd give me a piece and say, 'This is what freedom tastes like.' So I guess I chew gum to remember him and how lucky we are to live in this time, not back then," Claire replied.

"Whoa, ask a simple question, get a meaningful answer," Jake said.

"It's not just every building that has a story, Jake . . . every person has a story, too," Chevy interjected. "And that's because many battles were fought right here in our country."

As afternoon turned to evening, Jake started to think he'd be able to speak fluent German from manually translating so many pages. His mind was getting tired, but something was coming into focus for him.

"I think we may have something," Jake said, almost to himself.

The others turned to him.

"I noticed that several times the Germans—and this is in July 1942—refer to someone they think might be in the Scouts. Not sure what that means, but they call this woman *Brot*. It means 'bread' in German. They suspect her of giving out bread above the ration limit."

"I found a reference to *pain*, as well," Claire said. "It's *bread* in French. Here." Claire pointed to the paper in her hand.

Jake leaned in, forgetting for a moment that he couldn't read French.

"These are notes from one of the French policemen assigned to monitor potential members of the Resistance. In the note, they state they've been following the 'woman with the bread' and have observed her always writing in a red book. A chase ensued, but she disappeared inside the park."

"Red book? Are you sure it's not blue?" Sophie asked. "Does it say which park? Maybe this is a different one, not the Buttes-Chaumont."

"It says *red*," Claire answered. "But it doesn't mention the park. However, it *does* say the 19th *arrondissement*."

"Then it must be the Parc des Buttes Chaumont. It *must* be!" Jake said.

"That's great—but now we have two books, blue *and* red, to track down, and also, this fact still doesn't solve our problem with getting *into* the grotto to search for the books or clues to where they are," Ben said, gulping down the last of his tea.

"Chevy, can you help?" Claire asked.

"Sadly, no. The company doing the renovations is not cooperative and insists on an official police request."

"And the French police are not about to dig into something that will highlight their collaboration with the Nazis even though it was 70 years ago," Ben declared.

"You have a firm grasp on the political situation, young man."

"What do you think the reference to Scouts is?" Jake asked.

"I'm sure it means Éclaireurs Israélites de France," Claire responded.

"Translate?" Jake and Ben said in unison.

"Jewish Scouts of France. They ran camps for kids to learn Hebrew and rituals and things. But when their group was broken up by the Vichy government at the end of 1941, they transformed their mission to something heroic—actually *saving* kids," Claire explained.

"Well, whatever was happening in July 1942 in Paris involved Dahlia in some important way," Jake said. "Claire, do you know what was going on?"

"Yes, the roundup of foreign-born Jews," she said.

"And according to this article about that time," Ben said, tapping his tablet, "the 20th *arrondissement* was one of the districts in Paris that was home to a lot of foreign-born Jews—like Dahlia. Listen. Right now, we have to get into that grotto. Maybe what we need is a big distraction to draw the guards away."

"It just so happens we know someone who can help," Jake offered.

"We do?" Ben asked.

"Let's just say, there is more than one way to skin a cat," Jake grinned.

19

INTO THE WATER

A few minutes before 4:00 the next morning, Jake and Ben dressed in black and left Jenna's apartment. A dark-paneled van, rented by Chevy, was waiting for them on the street. Without a word, the two of them climbed into the back and positioned themselves on either side of an inflatable boat—the thick, rubber-walled kind used by the military. The amount of air required to fill a boat big enough to transport the two boys and a metal detector exceeded anything a small pump could handle. So they had purchased the craft, inflated it at a gas station, and stashed it in the van late the night before.

"OK, so let's review the plan one more time," Chevy said, when the boys were settled. "You'll be across the water by 4:45, as you won't need more than a couple of minutes to row. Take cover, and then move toward the grotto at sunrise, at which point the others will have already begun distracting the guards," Chevy said.

"Got it," the boys said. The streets of Paris were eerily quiet, and within a few minutes, they were approaching the park.

"I'm going to make a pass first, just to be sure," Chevy called over his shoulder from the driver's seat.

Jake felt the van loop slowly around the curved road that bordered the park near the lake.

"One minute to the drop-off point," Chevy said.

Jake and Ben fist-bumped.

"Now," Chevy said, bringing the van to an abrupt halt. As rehearsed, Jake threw the sliding door open and Ben launched the boat out of the van. Jake was right behind him, carrying his backpack and the large metal detector. Ben had dropped the boat face-up as if it were already in the water. Jake put his backpack and the metal detector into it as Ben shut the van door. Chevy was already pulling away from the curb when Ben and Jake each grabbed a handle of the boat and took off.

"Out and moving in 10 seconds. Not bad," Jake huffed, as he and Ben trotted down the grassy slope past patches of bright yellow flowers, crossed over the pathway, and continued a few more feet on lush green grass to the water's edge. Reaching the shore just after 4:30, the boys loaded the boat with their gear, pulled on their life jackets, and started paddling. As with nearly everything else they did, they rowed in perfect unison to the same beat—as if they were back home, playing together in the school orchestra. They saw a few fish under the water's surface, and some ducks and geese gliding silently across it; but otherwise there were no signs of life on the water or on either shore. When they reached the other side, Jake stepped into the water—ignoring the cold sting that radiated up to his knees—and dragged the front of the boat up onto the ground. Ben crawled out, keeping his feet dry.

"Thanks for the valet service," Ben grinned.

"You should have been in the front. The water wouldn't have gone so high on your legs." Jake pointed to the height difference between them.

"Sorry about that!" Ben helped pull the raft the rest of the way up onto the ground and under some trees. Then the boys climbed back into the boat to avoid sitting on the ground.

"Now we wait," Jake said.

"No, now we snack." Ben ripped open the Ziploc bags full of food Aunt Jenna had packed.

"Still thinking with your stomach?" Jake teased.

"Weren't you the one who said army guys always eat when they can?" Ben replied.

"True enough. My great-uncle did recall that about his service in the Irish Army. It's gotta be the same for soldiers everywhere. Eat and sleep when you can because you never know when you'll get the opportunity again."

"After buying all this last night, I've been craving it," Ben said. He opened a jar of gefilte fish and dipped a cracker into the minced whitefish.

"Cold fish at 5:00 a.m.?" Jake questioned.

"Breakfast of champions," Ben grinned.

"Sounds fishy," Jake replied.

"Easy pun—doesn't count. Are you *fin*-ished?" Ben asked.

Jake laughed and tried to get comfortable in the raft. The boys took turns, one trying to sleep while the other watched for danger, but in the end, the cold, excitement, and cramped quarters of the boat made any rest impossible.

"Can you imagine floating in the ocean in one of these? Like downed pilots from World War II?" Ben said.

"No. But then there are a lot of things I can't imagine from World War II," Jake replied.

Ben was silent for a moment.

"You're thinking about your family, aren't you?" Jake said.

"Yeah, my grandfather, my Zayde. He's 82 now, but he was just a 13-year-old boy, living in Hungary when Germany invaded. Within months, they rounded up the Jews in the provinces and sent them to Auschwitz—440,000 of them! Of his entire family, he was the only survivor. He had been transferred to Buchenwald."

"When did you learn all of this?" Jake asked, hoping not to press too hard.

"Right after I turned 13 and had my bar mitzvah. His memories came out like a flood. It was as though my turning 13 had reminded him of every detail of what it was like when *he* was that age, and he suddenly needed to talk about it. He even did a video interview for the Shoah Foundation."

"I hope that helped him," Jake said.

"I think it did. He told me a lot: He told me that he was one of only about a thousand children alive when the camp was liberated in 1945. He lied on the day he arrived at the camp, saying he was a 16-year-old. He was tall for his age. He said that his quick thinking saved him from being killed on the spot, and that he was worked really hard in a stone quarry. Every time I saw Zayde during that year, he talked and talked about it. And then one day, he just turned it off like a faucet. Suddenly, there were no more questions and no more answers. But I have to say, he seems much happier now."

Jake put his hand on Ben's shoulder. "I think your grandfather will be proud of you when he hears about what you've been doing here, don't you?"

"I think so. I really want to find what Dahlia left behind," Ben said. "It could be so important to a lot of people . . . even after all these years."

"*Especially* after all these years," Jake said, as dawn lit the sky.

20

THE EAGLE HAS LANDED

Bzzzzzzz. Jake's cell phone vibrated in his pocket.

"It's Sophie. Aunt Jenna says, 'Meow.'"

"OK, the protest in the park is ready to go!" Ben said.

"It's so nice of her to create a distraction for us. You're lucky to have such a great aunt, Ben."

"I am, aren't I," he grinned. "Listen, we should change now. It's light enough that our black clothes don't help—in fact, they might make us stick out more."

"Good point," Jake said. "We'll blend in a bit better in a crowd in the event we get off the island and need to disappear." He pulled off his black sweater and swapped out his black nylon running pants for blue jeans, then stuffed the black clothes into a plastic bag and tossed it into the raft. A few moments later, Jake's cell phone buzzed again. He glanced at the phone and laughed out loud.

"Aunt Jenna really came through. Look at this picture, taken right at the entrance to the park. The guards will be there in no time!" Jake held the phone up so Ben could see the picture of 10 people and more than a hundred cats. Jenna was in the middle, with Romeo on a leash. She held a sign that read "Save Our Squirrels and Birds and Bunnies by Finding Homes in the Country for Wild City Cats," with the French translation—or what Jake assumed must be the French translation—just below. Behind the feline mob, Jake could see a news van.

"I really didn't think her plan of smearing gefilte fish along the sidewalks north of the park would lure so many feral cats!" Jake said.

"She said she got the idea from a fellow cat lover who used to capture wild city cats and relocate them to farms where they could be useful in keeping rats and mice out of the barns. Cats were safely out of the city, squirrels and bunnies and birds were safer, and farmers were happy. Win-win-win," Ben beamed.

"Well, that should draw the guards' attention. People love cat videos," Jake said. "It'll probably go viral."

"Now it's *our* show time." Ben led Jake through the brush toward the grotto.

"I bet it won't take the guards long to realize it's a stunt and suspect something is up," Jake said. He glanced at his watch. "We have 10 more minutes, best case."

Ben led the way with the metal detector and entered the cave. They scanned the floor and walls with the detector.

"Found your drone," Ben said, as he brushed pieces of the destroyed helicopter off to the side of the floor.

Jake bent down and rummaged through the parts. "I'll grab the camera and the GPS tracker. They seem okay. But the rest of it will never fly again." He shoved the components into his pockets and followed Ben.

"Houston, we've got a problem," Ben called.

Jake caught up to find Ben standing over a small hole cut into the stone floor. "This is the general spot where Sophie said her Bubbe came with her mother and father before the war. It looks like someone's already found whatever was hidden here."

"And I think their names are Pierre and Michel. Remember when Sophie explained to the guards the importance of what we were looking for when she was at the police station? They must have come back here and decided to do some digging," Ben said.

"From the size of that hole, I think they may have found Dahlia's book," Jake said indignantly.

"Or books."

Heat radiated from Jake's neck. "Scoundrels."

"Nice throwback word choice. I might have gone with dirtbags. Let's go." Ben grabbed Jake by the arm and pulled him toward the boat, and a few moments later they were in the raft and paddling speedily toward the opposite shore. They met up with Chevy and the girls back at the van.

"Bad news," Jake told them. He explained what they'd discovered, and his suspicions as to the responsible parties.

"So now what? Chevy, can you arrest them?" Sophie asked.

"Maybe, but then I'd have to reveal that you trespassed," Chevy replied.

"The hole looked pretty fresh. We can probably assume they just discovered something there but haven't done anything with it yet," Jake said.

"So we watch them. See what they do and where they go?" Heather suggested.

"That could be difficult," Sophie said. "They could leave the park in any number of directions. We'd all have to watch a different side 24 hours a day." She looked like she was about to cry.

"Not necessarily," Jake said. "The construction company has cameras up and running to protect their equipment. They're probably connected to Wi-Fi. Ben can hack their system, giving us a view of their work trailer."

"How close do you need to be?" Claire asked.

"There is that small church across the street from the park. If I could get into that tower, it would be nice and high with a line of sight to the perimeter cameras. With the range extender from when we used the Wi-Fi drone, I can probably pick up the signal," Ben replied.

"Let's go then." Jake led the group down the street.

* * *

The clergyman was a bit resistant to the group's dragging equipment up to his belfry, but he relented after a healthy contribution to the donation box (courtesy of the money Jake received after finding the Irish treasure the summer before).

"Ben, do your magic quickly because we need to be at the mystery challenge bake today in 45 minutes," Heather reminded them.

"I'll be ready in five minutes," Ben replied, as his fingers flew across the tablet.

"Listen, guys. Heather, Ben, and I will be back as soon as possible. Chevy will drive us with Sophie in case the moped rider shows up again. Claire, please monitor the cameras, and if the guards go somewhere, try to follow them," Jake instructed.

"Cameras are up!" Ben pumped his fist in the air.

"Let's go bake," Heather called, already halfway out the door.

21

BAKE 5 AND MOPED MAN

"Baklava with handmade filo dough? Nobody makes filo dough by hand anymore," Ben grumbled, after Jacques announced the mystery-challenge instructions.

"Baklava is one of the oldest pastries in the world. It's always been made by hand," Jake replied.

"And people used to use carrier pigeons for mail and leeches for medicine."

"Hmm. I actually read that leeches are making a come-back—they help with certain nervous system disorders and also can prevent blood clots in surgery patients," Jake said.

"Good, because you probably picked up a few of them when you hopped into the lake this morning to pull the raft to shore," Ben laughed.

"Very funny, Ben." Jake casually lifted his pants and snuck a look at his ankles, just in case.

As the boys prepped their dough, Jake saw Heather moving swiftly back and forth between rolling her dough and slicing her butter. *I don't know how she does this all alone,* he thought. *Maybe some people just develop that way. Or maybe she really would be better off with a partner. I'm lucky that I can work with Ben. It's more fun—and much less pressure!*

"*Nut*withstanding the fact that I could sit here all day and *smell* the baklava," Jacques said, "it's time for our judges to *taste* your masterpieces."

Jake looked around at the other teams' tables. All had decent-looking baklava except the Norwegian team. Theirs was a gooey mess.

"Too much butter," Ben whispered, nodding toward their table.

Meredith and François approached Heather's table first.

"Good, crisp, flaky consistency. Appears to be baked perfectly," Meredith said, as she cut into Heather's pastry.

"It's nearly perfect," François said after taking a bite. "I would say it just needed one more turn of butter and dough."

"Thank you. I ran out of time to get the butter sliced and set," Heather admitted.

Next, the judges stopped at Jake and Ben's table. Meredith complimented the crispness of their pastry, just as she had when evaluating Heather's. François bit into their baklava and slowly chewed. His face scrunched up.

"It pains me to say it—"

Oh, no, we did something wrong! Jake thought.

"—but I think this is the best baklava I have ever tasted. *Oui*, even better than mine!" François exclaimed in a rare show of joviality.

The room erupted into applause and Jake exhaled with relief. Ben was stunned. He couldn't move a muscle, except for the corners of his mouth, which were stretched out—even farther than the boys' filo dough had been—into the biggest grin Jake had *ever* seen.

*　　*　　*

"Moped again at nine o'clock," Ben called out as the three of them walked down the steps of the building.

"Perfect. Heather, text Chevy and Sophie to be ready. We'll walk to the right, but slowly this time," Jake said. He was trying hard not to turn his head toward the moped.

They rounded the corner, but instead of going into the park, they continued down the street. As they reached the edge of the park, the street narrowed and became one-way. Cars were jammed in bumper to bumper on both sides.

"How do they pull out of their spaces when they're so jammed in?" Jake pointed at the few inches between cars.

"I read somewhere that people set their cars in neutral and when someone needs to leave, they gently tap on the bumper in front of them to make room," Ben said.

"Seems crazy to me. Is Red Helmet still behind us?" Jake asked.

"Yes." Ben held his phone up with the camera swiveled to see his own face, creating a makeshift rearview mirror.

Jake sent a text to Chevy. "Thirty seconds should be enough for them to get here, right?"

"Perfect," Ben said.

They slowed down as they neared the end of the block. Sophie appeared from around the corner, having jumped out of Chevy's car moments before.

Jake whistled, and they all scurried from in between the cars to stand in the middle of the road. They stood side by side and locked arms, forming a human roadblock.

The moped stopped dead.

"If he comes at us, we separate, okay? This is a bluff . . . not worth getting hurt over," Jake said, staring at the rider.

"It's working. He's turning around," Sophie said.

But as the moped turned around, Chevy's van appeared, blocking the rider from the other direction.

"Now!" Jake yelled, and the kids sprinted forward. At the same time, Chevy jumped out of the van and held up his badge. They saw the rider turn in every direction, desperately searching for an escape route. Boxed in, the rider killed the engine, pushed out the kickstand, and stepped off the bike.

Chevy and his impromptu posse encircled the rider.

"*Enlever le casque,*" Chevy commanded. "Take the helmet off."

The rider tugged the helmet up, revealing his face.

It was a young boy with a dark complexion and thick black hair. He moved into a karate stance and performed rapid-fire punches and kicks to the air.

"He's just a kid, like us," Sophie said.

"Take it easy. We're not looking to hurt you. We just want to know what you're doing. Do you speak English?" Jake asked.

"Yes, I do," the boy said with a heavy Spanish accent.

"Why are you following us?" Jake asked.

"*S'il vous plaît,* Jake, may I ask the questions? I think that's in my job description. I even have a badge for it. See?" Chevy grinned. "What's your name and where are you from, young man?"

"Felix Pérez. I live in the Navarra region in Spain," the boy replied, his voice cracking.

"No need to be afraid, Felix. I am not going to arrest you. Just tell me why you are interested in my friends here." Chevy put his hand on the boy's shoulder.

"I am a journalist," Felix answered.

"Aren't you kind of young for a journalist?" Jake asked. "Oops, sorry, Chevy."

"No, that's a good question, Jake. Well, Felix?"

"Yes, but I write for my school paper. I want to *be* a journalist, a real one, when I'm older. But my family does not have any money, so I need to get a scholarship. I read about what Jake did in Ireland and then again in Chicago. I figured an article about him, a kid who has done big things, would be the right story to win the scholarship."

Jake felt relieved about Felix now, but still confused. "You could have just called me or written to me," he said.

"*Si*, yes. I was going to do that, but then I learned about the baking contest, so I came here. It's close enough to Spain. I was just going to introduce myself, but then I decided to follow you for a while, to see what you were doing with your free time in Paris. I thought it would add a good human-interest aspect to the story."

"You've done your research, Felix. You certainly *sound* like a journalist," Sophie said.

Felix beamed. "*Gracias.* It appears you are, how you say, involved in another adventure? Something to do with that park?"

I like this kid. I think he's telling the truth, and maybe he can help us, Jake thought. "Why don't we get off the street and talk about this some more," Jake suggested, receiving a crisp head-nod from Chevy.

Chevy parked the van while the five of them sat down with Felix in a nearby café.

"Was that karate you were showing us?" Ben asked.

"*Si.* I only know a little. My town, it's not so safe. Sorry if I scared you."

"Did you ride that scooter all the way from Spain?" Claire asked.

"No. A truck driver who is a friend of mine gave me a ride up to Toulouse, south of Paris."

"Still, riding from Toulouse is a long way. Are you staying at a hostel?" Sophie asked.

Felix nodded.

Jake told Felix the story of the photograph, Sophie and his connection to her, and the Parc des Buttes Chaumont.

"That is incredible. It would be so amazing if you could

find these possessions and put them into the hands of their rightful owners," Felix said.

"That's the hope! I'm thinking we could use more help. What do the rest of you think?" Jake asked.

"Yes!" they all responded.

"It's settled then. Felix, do you want to join our cause?" Jake asked.

"*Si, gracias*—that would be *increíble.*"

"By the way, how'd the bake go?" Sophie asked.

"Very well. We were both at the top of the list. The Norwegian team tripped up: their soggy bottoms placed them last."

"Soggy bottom? Is that some sort of insult?" Sophie asked.

"No, their bottoms were really soggy. I mean, their pastry's bottom layer was too moist," Jake blushed.

"So *tomorrow* is the final bake?" Chevy asked.

"No, thankfully we have the day off. The other teams will get to practice while we try to steal back whatever the guards stole," Ben replied.

Jake called Claire and put her on speaker phone. "Any movement from the park?"

"Nothing. They come out to smoke about every 15 minutes, but neither of them has left the park yet."

"We should get some rest," Jake said.

"I'd like to learn some of Ben's hacking skills. Why doesn't Ben come back here," Claire suggested.

"I can put Felix's scooter in the van and drop him off at the church," Chevy said. "And while I'm out, I can get us some supplies."

"I'll come with you," Sophie said.

"Okay, Heather and I will order a bunch of cold sandwiches we can eat later, if we're still staking out the guards from the church," Jake said.

The group broke up, and after Jake and Heather called the waitress over to order, they got to talking.

"Ben is brilliant," Heather declared.

"Yes, he is." Jake took a sip of his iced tea. "He's gotten me out of more than a few scrapes with his wizardry."

"I think you're pretty clever too, though. I looked you up on the internet. As Felix said, it's quite impressive what you did in Ireland and Chicago."

Jake blushed. "You googled me?"

"I google everyone I meet. As head pastry chef for the palace, my father has a lot of access to the royal family and is concerned that others will try to take advantage of that," Heather replied.

"I guess that makes sense. People can be weird," Jake sighed.

"You okay? You've seemed distracted ever since we met." Heather's eyes had a genuine look of concern.

A great baker and *intuitive*, Jake thought. "I don't know. I used to take it for granted that I knew what I would be when I grew up. But this business with Dahlia and the past has me wondering who I am and what it could all mean for my future. I mean, I thought I was just Irish, and now I might be French and Jewish, too. It's all so confusing."

Heather was silent for a moment. "I think you might be putting too much weight on your family ancestry. After all, who your great-grandparents were doesn't determine who *you* are or what you'll be, does it? Look at this new connection as an opportunity to explore a culture rich with history and tradition. But in the end, you're still you. You'll be who you want to be, right? The past can't make you otherwise." Heather reached across the table and placed her hand on his.

"Thank you, Heather, that helps. Can't say I won't still be

a little distracted, though. It's a lot to process."

"I understand, but please try to point your distractedness toward the Dutch team. I'd rather they get spilled on instead of me," she giggled.

"Will do. Who do you think will win?"

"Not me," Heather said matter-of-factly. "I made a mistake thinking I could do this all by myself. Arrogance on my part to think my efficiency and creativity could make up for the lack of diversity in thought."

"Diversity in thought is a good way to put it. Having constructive opinions from other people can steer something from being dull and routine to something special," Jake replied.

"Not to mention the extra physical work. Nothing can replace a second pair of helping hands."

"Unless that pair of hands keeps spilling on their neighbor," Jake grinned.

"*Touché,*" Heather said as the waitress returned with the giant bags of food.

As they left the café, Chevy's van screeched to a halt in front of them.

The side door opened and Felix motioned with his hand. "Get in, you two—the guards are on the move!"

22

LEAPFROG!

"Jake and Heather, listen! As soon as Ben got back to the church, he and Claire spotted the guards walking toward their vehicle. That was just a few minutes ago," Chevy said, as he cut into traffic.

"Where are Claire and Ben now?" Jake asked.

"They jumped into a cab to follow the guards. They're texting us where they are every few minutes," Sophie replied.

Ding!

Jake glanced at his phone. "Green Ford Mondo. Hope you know what that is," he called out.

"There it is." Chevy pointed to a small aqua hatchback.

Ding!

Jake put his phone on speaker.

"Boy, did we luck out!" Ben said. "Our cab driver is a fan of spy movies, so we can trade positions back and forth between cars to avoid alerting them. We'll turn off at the next street and then run parallel for a few blocks over on Rue Sainte Joséphine."

Chevy expertly hung a few cars back from the guards.

"You do this a lot?" Jake asked.

"Used to. Now I handle mostly business crimes, so I don't do a lot of field work anymore," Chevy replied.

The green Ford turned onto Highway A13 toward Rouen and headed out of the city.

"We're right behind you if you want to go ahead." Claire's voice came over the speaker.

Chevy pressed the accelerator and sped past the guards. Jake ducked down in case they happened to look up at the paneled van as they passed.

Chevy and the taxi continued their game of auto leapfrog as the guards settled into what looked to be a lengthy drive.

"Where could they be going?" Jake muttered.

"I'm hoping whatever clue they found in the grotto—and please, let it be Dahlia's books!—is leading them, and us, somewhere helpful," Chevy replied.

"If not, Ben and Claire will have a very expensive cab bill and nothing to show for it," Heather said.

"It looks like we're going to Versailles. Could the Jewish families' treasures be hidden *there?*" Jake asked.

"Doubtful. Versailles was a German stronghold, so it would have been tough to hide anything in the palace," Chevy replied.

"I have a bad feeling about this. It doesn't make sense that Dahlia and the Resistance would have lugged people's stuff this far out of Paris, does it?"

"Good point," Chevy said. "Look, they're getting off the highway." He signaled and followed.

Jake called Claire. "They just exited, so you'll need to circle back since you were ahead of them."

Chevy accelerated to keep the Ford in their sights. "This is the industrial part of Paris. Not much here but factories and some housing."

"They're stopping!" Jake pointed as the guards pulled up to an old warehouse.

"What's that sign say?" Jake pointed to a worn billboard

mounted on the warehouse's wall.

"It says Paris Security Systems. Must be where their offices are or maybe where they store supplies," Sophie replied.

Chevy pulled to the curb, just short of the factory's entrance, and leapt out of the van, with Jake, Sophie, Heather, and Felix right behind him. They crept along a brick wall parallel to the street until they reached the entrance. Jake peered around the corner to see the guards leaving their car and entering the dilapidated building.

"They have a book—and it's blue!" Jake whisper-yelled. "Let's go!" Jake ran to the guard's car and ducked down behind it, watching the metal door for any signs of movement. He heard the crunch of gravel behind him, signifying that Chevy, Sophie, Heather, and Felix had joined him.

"Should we go in, Chevy?" Sophie whispered.

"Not yet. Let's go around back and see if we can take pictures through the windows. This may only be a pit stop. We don't want to confront them until we know what's inside."

Just as they reached the other side of the building, they heard the rattling sound of an old motor starting up.

"They're leaving!" Chevy exclaimed. "Let's go!"

When they skidded to a stop at the front corner of the building, they saw that Michel was in the driver's seat and Pierre was loading shovels in the back of the hatch. Heather quickly switched her phone from picture mode to video mode.

"They came for supplies to dig!" Sophie said. "They must know where the treasure is!"

They piled into the van as quickly as they could, preparing to resume the chase. But when Chevy turned the key, the car made a sickening click-click sound and nothing more.

"Ugh! What a time for car trouble!" Heather said. "Now we've lost them." She slapped her hand against the door.

Jake grinned. "No we haven't."

23

AH-HAH!

"When we knelt beside their car before going into the building, I taped the GPS tracker from our broken helicopter under their bumper and set it up so the device would alert any movement to Ben's phone," Jake said.

"Good thinking, Jake!" Sophie exclaimed.

"I'm impressed, too," Chevy said with a smile. "OK, I just used my car-service app and ordered a van to pick us up. It should be here soon."

They hadn't been in the van for more than a minute when they heard Jake's phone.

Ding!

"Ben texted. Here's the address where the GPS tracker stopped." Jake held his phone up to show Chevy, who then conveyed the address to the driver in French.

"I've got a bad feeling about this," Chevy said, as the car turned onto a residential street. He shouted something to the driver and suddenly the car accelerated down the block and turned at the corner.

"Hey, you're passing the house where Ben said the signal stopped," Jake called, as he turned around in his seat.

"We don't need to stop. I know that house. It's Lieutenant Boucher's—the officer who wants to be the new *directeur* of police. I came here once for a holiday party. I think he wanted to show off his fancy house and flaunt the fact that the commissioner had attended his party."

Jake bit his bottom lip. "So the guards knew we were following them, ditched us, and then came straight to Boucher's house, probably with whatever they found in the grotto!"

Jake called Ben and put him on speaker. "How long was the signal at that house?"

"The guards stayed there about 20 minutes and now seem to be on their way back to the park," Ben replied.

"So, odds are, they gave Boucher whatever they found. He must have made a deal with them after they all met at the police station, when they wanted to arrest Sophie," Jake said. "We need to go in and get whatever they brought there. Chevy, can you remember the layout of the house?" Jake started pulling up satellite imagery of the area on his phone.

"Jake." Ben's voice was crystal clear over the speaker. "Jake, I know that tone. But think about it: this is a by-the-book senior member of a foreign city's police force."

"*Oui*, your friend is right, Jake. We do not know Boucher's intent or why the guards are meeting him," Chevy said.

"Come back and we'll figure something else out, Jake," Claire added softly.

Fighting tears, Jake agreed.

After a silent drive back, the group was reunited at the church. Sophie's charm—coupled with a nice selection of food from the café—had convinced the caretaker to allow them full access to the building for the night. Their own café sandwiches sat untouched, as the solemn mood had stifled everyone's appetite.

"Why would Boucher care about the grotto finding?" Claire asked.

"I don't know. I had assumed he was taking the guards'

side because I was supporting Sophie or because it was the law—or both. But this is different. We're missing something," Chevy said.

"The answer is in what they found. I know it," Jake grumbled.

"So what would Dahlia do?" Ben asked.

"She'd take back the book," Claire said.

"But for that to work, we'd have to know when he'd be carrying it!" Jake said.

"Whatever he is up to with the guards must be important if he's teaming with bullies like them. I bet he carries the book with him wherever he goes," Ben suggested.

"I agree," Sophie said.

"Your best bet is the Métro or right after he gets off the Métro near the station," Chevy said. "His daily schedule is a model of consistency. You can set your watch by it. He exits the Métro at 8:15 a.m. and walks through the station door at 8:25. People around the station joke about it. Your job will be to take that book from him between the Métro and the police station. But remember, no one gets hurt."

"Understood. And I know exactly how we'll do it," Claire said, pulling out a piece of paper. Jake started to say something, but Ben put a hand gently on his knee. *Ben's right. This is her turf.* Jake remembered his great-uncle's leadership lessons. *The hardest part of leadership is knowing when to follow.*

24

MISSION: POSSIBLE

Jake's neck itched from the scratchy corduroy jacket he was wearing. They hadn't had a lot of time to select clothes from the thrift shop the night before, as it had been about to close. He had chosen black pants, a simple gray button-down shirt, the brown corduroy jacket, and of course, a beret.

Jake bent over and pulled his violin out of its case. He looked at Ben, who had similarly disguised himself with brown pants, a faded blue T-shirt, and a black faux-leather jacket. The clothes were all well-worn, and Claire had concurred that the boys looked French enough to not warrant a second glance.

Hopefully, nobody will notice we're playing with expensive violins, Jake thought as he and Ben leaned up against the police station wall. Jake used his foot to push his open case onto the sidewalk and threw some euros into it as seed money. He nodded to Ben, and the boys started playing Mozart's Violin Concerto no. 3. Despite the hustle and bustle on the city street, their performance was impressive enough to draw a small crowd.

Perfect, a few more people and the sidewalk will be properly blocked, Jake thought. Again he nodded to Ben, and they started their second number, Paganini's Caprice no. 24.

Although the piece was more obscure, its fast tempo yet soulful sound always got people's attention.

Out of the corner of his eye, Jake saw a bald man emerging from the nearby Métro staircase—it was Boucher, right on time. Jake tapped his foot, and he and Ben immediately started playing the theme from *Mission Impossible*.

DAH-DAH da da, DAH-DAH da da . . . the familiar tune on the violins echoed off the wall. The crowd clapped with delight as they recognized the opening of the famous film's score.

Due to the size of the gathering, Boucher had to swing wide on the sidewalk and step into the gutter. A group of French teens emerged from the subway and paced themselves, walking a few yards behind Boucher. In his peripheral vision, Jake saw a teenage girl walk straight toward Boucher. Just then, Felix, on his moped, rounded the corner. He rang the little bell on his handlebars, causing Boucher to turn his head toward the street.

Jake watched as the girl's hand darted out from her bulky coat, like a snake's tongue tasting the air. Jake stifled a gasp as the cop spun around. Boucher had felt it, felt the object being lifted from his possession. Boucher grabbed the girl by the jacket and pulled her near him. She let out a cry as she held the object above her head, away from Boucher's reaching arm. It was a blue leather-bound book.

The group of teens following Boucher started yelling at him and shoving him. The crowd turned their heads to see the commotion behind them. Boucher was now in the street, and although Jake couldn't understand the French, he assumed the teens were yelling at the man to leave the girl alone.

Boucher, outnumbered and flustered, shouted back and pulled out his badge. The teens stepped back as one and put their hands up. Jake's eyes fixated on the book still held aloft by the girl. As Boucher closed in on her, Felix, who had turned around and come back up the street, motored past with Claire now riding on the back of the scooter. The girl in the bulky coat flicked her wrist. The book sailed perfectly and was plucked from the air by Claire as the moped sped away before Boucher could even turn around.

One of the kids then dropped a magician's smoke ball, causing a short burst of smoke and a flash of light, lasting just long enough for all of them to disappear into the subway station. Jake grinned as he and Ben grabbed their violin cases and darted after them down the Métro stairs.

The entire episode, Claire's plan, had been implemented with incredible precision and accuracy.

Wow. Claire would have made a great Resistance fighter had she been around back then, Jake decided.

25

WHICH SPOT?

"Ten euros!" Ben said. "Not bad for 10 minutes' work." He dumped the loose change from Jake's case. "More donations for the church."

"Our first professional gig was pretty exciting, too! I don't think we'll ever play again where the stakes are so high: that book with information on people's priceless valuables," Jake said.

Sophie said nothing. She sat in a corner of the church, reading through the recovered book as fast as she could. *What's in there? Tell us, Sophie.* Jake silently urged her to read even faster than her blazing five-pages-per-minute speed.

Sophie sighed, her eyes still glued to the book.

"What's the matter?" Jake asked, as the others gathered around.

"Well, as we expected, the book's mostly an inventory with lists of furniture, paintings, jewelry, etc., and the people who owned them, along with their addresses. People whom Dahlia helped escape aren't mentioned," she said.

"So now we just have to find the location of all these items and the *red* book," Jake said.

"*Oui,*" Sophie answered. "But there's more. A part of this book contains Dahlia's journal. And it mentions that there is treasure stored in the family's grandfather clock below the *something-or-other* spot in Paris."

"Below the *what* spot in Paris?" Jake asked.

"I don't know—that word is smudged!"

"But this is great news! The *red* book with the families' names must be inside that grandfather clock!" Jake exclaimed.

"Is that all that's in the book?" Heather asked.

"No, one more thing. There is mention of fear of the system falling apart—members disappearing. And it refers to a French policeman named Boucher, followed by one word: *serpent.*"

"*Serpent?* Translate?" Jake and Ben said together.

"It's a synonym in French . . . for 'traitor,'" Sophie replied.

For a moment, no one said a word.

"Boucher's relative?" Jake asked, breaking the quiet. "Let's text Chevy and find out."

"On it!" Ben said. Within five minutes, they had their answer: YES, HIS GRANDFATHER. MEMBER OF POLICE NATIONALE IN PARIS, 1935-1946. DIED IN 1955, AGE 55, OF PNEUMONIA AND WHAT DOCTORS NOW KNOW WAS EARLY-ONSET DEMENTIA.

Jake was the first to speak again. "Maybe Boucher's grandfather told Boucher's father about being in the police force and knowing about some hidden treasure."

"Right! And maybe Boucher's father didn't believe him," Sophie said, "if he told him while he was suffering from memory issues. But maybe Boucher's father shared the story with his son anyway."

"Right! Okay, so here's what we know so far," Jake said. "One: Boucher read the blue book—and most likely made a copy for safekeeping. Two: He now has *confirmation* from a second source—us—that there are precious possessions hidden somewhere in Paris. And three: He knows that his grandfather was actually a traitor, responsible for making members of Dahlia's underground group disappear."

"Okay, what will Boucher do now that he knows the story is real and that his grandfather worked with the Nazis?" Heather asked.

"Maybe he wants to find the treasure to help right his grandfather's wrong?" Ben suggested.

"That would be fine, as long as we get the red book with the family names," Sophie said.

"Agreed, but if he finds it and destroys the treasure and the red book, all we'll have is an uncorroborated old book." Jake slammed his fist into the pew.

"Translate," Claire said.

"Uncorroborated, meaning there would be no other proof that the blue book is true—and that Boucher's grandfather assisted the Nazis," Jake clarified.

"Then *we* have to find the hidden possessions first to get the red book and to tell the whole story—the *real* story about Boucher's family," Claire added.

"Since he's probably afraid that his family is going to be disgraced, he just became more than a nuisance. Now he's actually dangerous," Ben said.

Jake nodded. "From here on out, nobody goes anywhere by themselves, and we always leave a message saying where we are going and how long we will be gone. Does the book give any other clues as to where that spot might *be?*"

Sophie leafed to the middle of the book. "Right here! Dahlia talks about *fantôme*, or at least I think that's what it says. The ink ran a little, so the word isn't clear."

"Translate?" Ben and Jake said in unison.

"*Ghost* or *phantom*," Claire replied.

"In a war, *that* could mean anything," Ben said.

"Let's put it in context. These were people sneaking around at night, taking possessions and hiding them. What about the word *phantom* fits?" Jake asked.

"Didn't the phantom in *The Phantom of the Opera* have a secret lair below the Opera House? Could that be where the heirlooms are?" Heather offered.

"I think the musical came out in the 1980s, so it couldn't have been referenced during World War II. I can look up any other versions." Ben pulled out his tablet.

"*The Phantom of the Opera* was first a book, published in 1910 by Gaston Leroux," Sophie said.

"Sorry, Ben, my cousin is faster than the internet," Jake said.

"No problem! And listen to this: there was a movie by that name that came out in 1926!" Ben said, smiling.

"So there are *two* references from before the war?" Jake said. "This is getting more plausible now."

"What about the ghost stations of the Métro? I read about them. They were used before the war but then closed when the rail staff were called up to fight," Felix said.

"Good idea, but I've been over every meter of them. There's nothing there," Claire replied.

"Okay, then. I'm thinking we should check out the Opera House. It says here," Jake said, reading over Ben's shoulder, "that 'due to the wet ground, there is a large cistern in the basement. During construction, they had to build a double basement to keep the pillars dry.' Perhaps in the space between the foundations they stored stuff!"

"I agree. We should check out the Opera House," Claire chimed in. "They've probably had a ton of people traipsing through there like the ghost stations, but you never know. They may have missed the area *between* the double foundations."

"Looks like there's a matinée, the ballet *La Bayadère*, in two hours with just 10 tickets left," Ben read from his computer.

"I wonder if it's the Rudolf Nureyev interpretation," Claire said.

Everyone turned to look at her.

"You know *ballet?*" Ben's eyebrow raised.

"No. Um, ahem, not really," Claire stammered. "I just like Rudolf's backstory. He defected from the former Soviet Union and escaped the KGB. It's just the spy stuff, as you would say, that I like."

"Interesting. Okay, then, let's order the tickets," Jake said. "Listen, everybody. Ben and I need to grab some things. We'll meet you at the entrance in 90 minutes."

* * *

Jake's heart thumped in his chest as their taxi pulled up to the front of the neo-baroque-style building, adorned with marble columns, friezes, and statues.

"This was on my list to tour. It's too bad we'll be searching the basements instead of the public areas," Jake said to Ben as they trotted up the stairs to join the others.

The kids filed in one by one as the attendant scanned the tickets they had downloaded onto their phones. Behind the attendant was a security guard, who gave a cursory look inside Jake's backpack and Heather's purse.

"This is way cooler in person than the photographs in my guidebook," Ben said, gazing at the gilded lobby. The grand marble staircase led to an extravagant landing, then split into two stairways that headed in opposite directions toward ornate column-lined balconies. Chandeliers, sconces, and *torchères* illuminated the magnificently painted ceiling depicting gods, goddesses, and muses. Jake snapped a few pictures with his phone—knowing it would never look the same on the screen as it did in real life—and then continued past the stairways and headed for a roped-off area. Everyone followed.

*   *   *

"Did you guys decide how we're going to sneak into the basement?" Sophie asked.

"We did," Ben said. Ben and Jake pancaked themselves against the staircase so as to be out of the main sightline of the ticket takers and guards.

"Come stand around us and act like you're looking at your playbills," Jake said.

The group stood in a semicircle in front of the boys, and Jake and Ben rolled up their pants to reveal pieces of plastic taped to their legs.

"What is all of that?" Claire asked.

"A cheap drone that we disassembled so we could smuggle it in," Ben said.

Ben and Jake winced as they pulled the tape off, leg hair accompanying each piece of drone.

Within a few minutes, the eight-inch drone was reassembled and ready to fly. Ben's fingers were a blur as he programmed the flight path on his tablet.

"This is smart. Very smart. Everyone will be watching the drone fly while we sneak away." Claire nodded her head in approval.

"It's on a two-minute delay. Let's leave it here on the floor, and we'll go to the other side of the staircase so we're not around when it takes off," Jake said.

The gang worked their way through the throngs of last-minute arrivals that were heading up the stairs. A gasp from the opposite side of the stairs signaled that their drone had taken flight. Jake glanced up as the drone weaved in and out of the columns on the second floor. As expected, the guards ran toward the drone, not realizing that its flight could be controlled from anywhere in the room—or anywhere in the world, for that matter.

"Quickly now," Jake said, ducking under the velvet ropes. They arrived at a locked door leading to the backstage area.

"I've got this," Claire said. "You're not the only one who can pick a lock. I have to do it to access some of the Catacomb tunnels." Claire nudged Jake out of the way, brandishing her small tools. Within seconds, the door was open. Jake patted Claire as he walked past her. The orchestral music drifted in from the auditorium.

"Sounds like the ballet has started. Let's move quickly before anyone sees us. This way," Ben pointed, reading from his tablet. After navigating through two more locked doors, they found themselves looking down a long, dark stairway.

"Feels wet. We must be nearing the cistern," Claire said.

Jake handed out LED flashlights from his backpack and they descended slowly.

"This is pretty amazing," Felix said. The stairway they were on opened onto a platform, and beyond it was a massive underground lake. Their flashlight beams were not strong enough to reach the other side, creating the impression of an endless body of water.

"Here is a little-known fact: The fire department in Paris practices their underwater rescues down here sometimes," Claire said.

"Wow. And I can see where the inspiration for *The Phantom of the Opera* came from. This underground lake is spooky. I can almost see the phantom rowing his boat," Ben said.

Heather shuddered. "Don't creep me out, Ben. I think I just heard an oar splashing in the water."

"Okay, okay, now you're creeping *me* out. Listen, if I'm reading this right," Jake said, training his flashlight on the map, "the water drains into this cistern from around the columns and then is pumped out. The pumps have to be maintained, which would have been a job the French continued during the war. I don't see some Nazi down here schlepping hoses and greasing bearings. That means there was the potential to hide stuff," Jake added, moving cautiously toward the edge of the platform, searching the wall with his light and sweeping the beam systematically across the surface.

"Here we go." Jake opened a short metal door and climbed into the next room. A steady loud buzz of machinery signaled the presence of pumps. A large electrical box adorned with gauges sat in the middle of the room, and pipework from the cistern room disappeared into the wall on the other side. "Well, I have to admit, I *was* hoping to open that door and see a big grandfather clock, as well as the other heirlooms. This is just so very . . ."

"Anticlimactic?" Ben finished Jake's sentence.

"Exactly. Let's look around for some sort of passageway," Jake said.

The gang spread out and spent several minutes scouring the floor and walls.

"Nothing," Claire said finally.

"We'd better get out of here and rethink this," Ben suggested. "But first, let's see the ballet. I mean, we have tickets, right?" Everyone agreed.

"Good timing," Felix said. "According to the playbill, the intermission has just started."

The group scaled the steps leading out of the cistern and wound their way through the basement until they found a service door exit into the lobby. Once in the auditorium, they easily found their seats. Jake eyes were on the dancers, but his mind was elsewhere. *The Opera House didn't pan out, but at least I've found my family. And that's huge*, he thought.

Just then, one of the dancers performed a *grande jeté*, leaping into the air with athleticism and joy. *I know just how he feels*, Jake thought.

26

A VIEW FROM THE TOP

"We're out of leads and I'm out of gas. We need to clear our heads," Jake said.

"We could eat," Ben replied.

"I'm shocked!" Jake replied, laughing.

"I agree with Jake," Heather said. "We need to refresh our minds by *not* focusing on this puzzle. How about the Eiffel Tower? The baking show gave us passes to skip the line, enough for families of contestants, so we have plenty." Heather opened her satchel to show them the tickets.

"Food," Ben grunted.

"Both," Sophie replied. "There is a good sandwich place near the tower. We can grab some sandwiches to go and eat them while we look at the city lights. At this time of day, the view is spectacular."

A short time later, they were bypassing the ticket line and cramming into the lift.

"What's in that pink box?" Ben asked Claire.

"It's a surprise," she said.

The elevator stopped and the group found a spot near the northeast corner to look out over the city.

Claire opened the pink box she'd been carrying. "I hope

you haven't eaten *too* much pastry this week because I have a real treat."

"Mmm, this is extra-terrific because we didn't have to make it and get judged on it," Ben said, pulling out a gigantic multilayered rectangular pastry and taking a bite. "Wow, this is wonderful! Everybody, you've got to get in on this!"

"Best napoleons in Paris!" Claire beamed as she handed out the rest of the pastries.

"How very French of us," Jake said.

"Actually, napoleons aren't French," Sophie corrected. "Although they share the same name as the French leader, napoleons are named after the city of Naples in Italy, which is where they were invented."

"True, but Napoleon did make something famous in France. Any guesses as to what?" Claire asked.

When everyone shook their heads no, she said, "The Catacombs. He was so envious of Rome's stature in Europe and how popular *their* Catacombs were with tourists that he had some of the quarry tunnels in Paris cleaned up for sightseers in the city."

"Well, these napoleons are great. No bones about it!" Ben licked the last of the pastry cream from his fingers as the others groaned.

"I think we should go back and talk with my Bubbe," Sophie suggested. "I mean, I love it up here, talking and joking—"

"And don't forget *eating*," Ben said, just beating Felix to a broken piece of pastry stuck to the side of the box.

"But it will be after 11:00 by the time we get there," Heather said.

"If she's not awake now, she will be eventually. Ever since Jake and Ben arrived, she hasn't been able to sleep through the night. Her mind races with the hope that she may find her sister, Naomi."

133

Oh, poor thing. After all these years, to have her hopes be so high again, Jake thought. *We have just got to do it!*

When they arrived at Sophie's apartment, Esther was indeed awake in her chair, reading and eating rugelach.

"Bubbe, you're eating pastries so late at night?" Sophie asked. She had taken a moment to introduce everyone, but now she wanted her curiosity satisfied.

Esther's eyes brightened. "Ah, rugelach in the wee hours. I don't know why, but ever since Jake showed me his photo, I've been thinking . . . and remembering. And this rugelach," she said, holding the cookie aloft, "certainly brings back warm memories of my mama. I would hear her enter our apartment late at night smelling like a bakery. Often, she'd have a box of warm rugelach with her."

Sophie's head spun and her eyes locked with Jake's. "Bubbe, do you know what bakery she went to?"

"*Oui. La Patisserie de Marionettes.*"

"*Fantôme* was wrong! It was *fantoche*—another word for 'puppet'!" Sophie cried.

"The Puppet Bakery!" Claire exclaimed.

"The *sweetest* spot in Paris—not the *wettest!*" Ben added, filling in the missing word from Dahlia's journal.

"That's definitely it! The French police and the Germans always saw Dahlia with bread, remember?" Jake said. "*Pain* and *Brot!*"

"And if the Resistance operated out of a bakery, they might have been able to get passes that allowed them to be out after curfew, so they could start work in the bakery in the early morning," Claire said.

"That makes sense," Jake said, tapping Claire's arm.

"The bakeries will be opening soon. We don't have much time to check this theory out." Sophie looked at the time on her phone.

134

"Let's not sneak in. Let's try to talk our way in. All we want to do is look around. If we see something, we'll play it by ear," Jake suggested.

It was after 4:00 when they got to the bakery, where, as they had expected, the lights were on. They knocked loudly on the door until a middle-aged woman appeared. Her hair was tucked into a net and she had a full-length apron on, already coated with flour. Jake's gaze went straight to her neck, where a gold Star of David glistened in the fluorescent light. *A good sign*, he thought.

27

SWEET SPOT

Through the glass, Sophie spoke to the woman in French, and after a moment the woman unlocked and opened the door.

"Thank you for letting us in. I think you will find our story important," Jake said. He then stepped back so Sophie could continue. Speaking quickly and without hesitation, Sophie explained what they were doing. When she showed the woman Jake's photograph and the book of inventory lists that had been hidden in the grotto, the woman motioned for them to follow her into the kitchen.

"Look, a French oven. Puts steam into the chamber for moisture so you don't have to do a bain-marie," Ben whispered.

"Nice. We could use one of those," Jake replied.

"I have to keep baking but please, look around," the woman told them. She motioned to a staircase that led to the basement.

"Thank you," Jake called back as they descended the stairs. The basement was dark and musty. Bags of flour and other ingredients were strewn about. The room wasn't large, definitely not as big as the bakery upstairs.

"This is interesting," Jake said, pointing to another set of stairs at the back of the room. The stairs were double wide and led up to a pair of horizontal doors, like a massive hatch at the top of a boat ladder.

"I bet they lead to the alley. Explains how they get the big bags of flour down here. Could easily move furniture through there!" Ben said quickly.

"Floors and walls. We scour every inch," Jake said.

"Let's try something else. Go close the upstairs door and turn off the light," Felix said.

Without asking any questions, Heather climbed the stairs and shut the door.

Good crew. They don't question each other's ideas, but simply support them. Jake beamed with appreciation.

Once Heather was back in the basement, Felix took out a book of matches. "Switch off the light and everyone be still." He struck a match and held it steady in his hand. The flame flickered a bit toward the back wall.

"A draft. Great idea!" Claire said.

Felix moved away from where the flame had flickered and struck another match. He repeated the process until he was up against the basement's east wall.

"Turn on the lights, *por favor*," he said.

Jake squinted as the sudden light flooded his pupils.

"There is a draft here. Very little but steady." Felix rubbed his hands along the grout between the field stones that made up the wall.

"What made you think of using the matches?" Ben asked.

"I like to stream old films. There was a movie once where they did that to escape a mine," Felix answered.

"If Dahlia and the Resistance really came in this way," Claire said, "then there must be some way of opening it." She approached the wall and started pushing on the stones.

"Any of the stones turn?" Jake said. *Maybe it's like the Clochan in Ireland.*

"Doesn't seem like it," Claire replied.

"I know it's been a long time and the floor could have been repaired, but I don't see any drag marks. Maybe the door lifts like a garage door?" Heather suggested.

"Good idea," Felix said. "The draft was near the top, so maybe that's where a hinge connects it." He knelt down, and Jake joined him on the floor. He opened his trusty Leatherman to the longer knife blade.

"It will destroy any sharpness, but let's see." Jake dragged the blade along the floor where it met the wall. At first, the blade left scratches in the cement floor, but after a few feet, it sank into the wall.

"Move this stuff!" He waved at boxes and flour bags propped against the wall. The others made quick work of the obstacles, and Jake continued to drag his knife along the crack until it reached the corner.

"If that's the width of the door, they could have easily gotten furniture through. Looks to be two meters," Heather said.

"But how would you lift it up? You can't get a pry bar under there," Ben said.

"You know a lot of old garage doors have a spring-loaded pivot system. Maybe push from the top while pulling from the bottom," Jake suggested.

Ben grabbed a broom from the corner of the basement. He placed the handle against the wall about a foot below the ceiling. With a grunt he leaned into the broom. Claire came over and pushed on his back to add force.

CREAK!

What a beautiful sound! Jake thought. The wall at the floor gapped open about an inch.

"Oh my goodness—it's really opening!" Heather said, getting on her knees to admire the gap.

"I'm afraid that's as far as it's going," Ben huffed.

"I'm sure the hinges are rusted shut. Drag a few bags of flour back over here, we need leverage," Jake said as he manhandled a bag over to the wall. He stopped about a foot away from the gap. Sophie and Felix placed another bag on top of his.

"Okay, Archimedes, use your broom." Jake motioned for Ben to come closer.

Ben wedged the handle in the one-inch space between the wall and the floor. "Give me a lever long enough and a place to stand and I'll lift the earth," Ben chuckled. With the flour bags as fulcrum, he pushed down on the broom. A loud metallic groan echoed in the small basement as the wall began to rise. When it had pivoted to reveal about two feet of open space, it stopped.

"That's it. It won't budge anymore," Ben said.

"It's enough. Let's go!" Jake flipped on his flashlight and climbed into the chamber.

28

AFTER ALL THESE YEARS

Jake choked on the musty, dank air. *Probably the first person to breathe it in 70 years.* He absently brushed dirt from his pants as his flashlight panned the room. The light bathed row after row of ghostly shapes, pieces of furniture covered with sheets and standing like an ancient army that was ready to come to life.

"Oh, my." Sophie was through next and stood beside Jake.

He felt her fingers wrap around his, and they stood in silence for a moment. "We did it," Jake whispered as he squeezed her hand.

"Jackpot," Ben said. One by one the others joined them inside the room.

"I see some oil lanterns over here. Do you have any matches left?" Claire asked.

Felix trotted over and helped Claire light a few lanterns.

"Got to love petroleum products. Eighty years later and it still lights—like a Hanukkah miracle," Ben commented.

"It seems they carved little ledges into the limestone walls for the lanterns." Claire motioned with her flashlight. Further inside, a two-foot by two-foot square had been cut into the wall.

"Let's light this place up and look for Bubbe's clock!" Sophie said.

The others quickly distributed the lights throughout the room until a soft glow illuminated the massive storage area. Returning to the entrance, the group stood silently for a minute to admire their find.

"This room looks to be nearly 300 feet long, based on that last lamp," Ben said.

Heather was the last to return. "I found a tunnel on the far side!" she told them. "It might lead to another way in here. But I didn't want to check it out alone."

"Let's spread out and see what's in here first." Jake took Sophie by the hand. *I want to experience this with her. My family.* He wiped a tear, gritty with limestone dust, from his cheek.

"I found the art section!" Claire called, and the others quickly moved to join her. She lifted a sheet to reveal stacks of paintings.

"That's a Cézanne!" Jake said. He picked up the painting and found yet another Cézanne behind it. "I bet there are dozens of famous lost works here."

"Look, there is writing on the back. It says '*Hayim Moshe Goldberg, Item 16,*'" Felix read. "And it has his address!"

"What's this?" Jake asked, as he touched an ornate brass pot.

"That's a Russian samovar, used to make hot water for tea. The family probably came to France sometime in the early 20th century to escape the pogroms—violent riots against Jews—in the Russian Empire," Sophie said softly.

"Someone saved a bottle of goo?" Heather asked, picking it up to get a closer look.

"Don't drop it—who knows what might be hidden inside. Could be gems. I heard that sometimes people hid stuff in gloppy food items because they knew that the Nazis didn't want to get their uniforms dirty and wouldn't do a careful search," Ben said.

"Here's a Torah from the Agoudas Hakehilos Synagogue," Sophie murmured. She ran her hand over its decorative silver case. *"Très belle."*

"OK, I think this is all too much to take in at once," Ben said, "so let's focus and first look for the grandfather clock."

Everyone agreed and dispersed again throughout the room. Jake paused when he found a piano. Tucked inside the piano bench was sheet music—easy pieces for a child to learn. He placed his fingers gently on the keys and closed his eyes. *I can almost hear the music . . . Of course, the child who played this piano would be around 80 now.*

"I found some clocks!" Ben called.

Sophie was the first to sprint over to him.

"Bubbe told me that their clock was 19th-century French," Sophie said, "with a painted pine case decorated with delicate bouquets of pink and white flowers, an enamel face, and an embossed brass pendulum. It was signed in front and on the clock face by, wait a minute—I had to write this down—Ferret à La Châtaigneraie. She adored that clock. It took her years to sleep through the night again without hearing the gong."

"I found it!" Felix shouted.

"French writing on the front," Ben confirmed. "The name matches exactly."

"Oh, I can't believe it! Bubbe is going to cry. She's just going to cry when we return this to her." Placing her hand gently against the glass door that protected the pendulum and gearing from the elements, she flipped the latch. The clock's door swung open. She felt around the sides and back and then got on her knees and rapped her knuckles on the base.

"Sounds hollow," Jake said, breathing for the first time in what felt like several minutes. He opened the flathead screwdriver attachment on his Leatherman and handed it to Sophie. "Here." Reaching into his pocket, he added, "Take my small flashlight, too."

She wedged the screwdriver's flat edge in between the clock's baseboard and side wall and pried carefully. The board popped out, sending seven decades of dust flying into the air.

"There's a red book in here!" Sophie exclaimed, pulling out the leather-bound volume. "There are also letters! They look like they are from Bubbe's papa. Dahlia must have saved them. Bubbe will be *so* happy to read letters from her father," Sophie said, clutching the red book to her chest.

"Is that it? I mean, are Bubbe's sisters' names in there?" Jake knelt beside Sophie.

"*Oui*. It lists their new names and the matching names of the families that took them in and . . . oh, my goodness!"

"What?" Jake asked.

"Miriam went to Switzerland."

"And Naomi?"

"Spain," Sophie answered. "Let me read some more." Jake, Ben, Heather, Claire, and Felix waited expectantly; no one said a word.

After a few minutes, Sophie was ready to speak. "Most of the diary has the names—real and false—of the children and adults that Dahlia's group escorted from Paris to the south, or which Christian or Jewish family they were placed with in Paris if they couldn't travel. There are hundreds of names listed here," Sophie said. "The handwriting is hasty, as if she were in a terrible hurry. But she explains the process completely. Dahlia learned—almost too late—that there was to be a massive roundup of foreign-born Jews in Paris on July 16th and 17th, 1942. More than 12,000. In order to help save as many people as possible, her group—which covered the 20th *arrondissement*—reached out to all of their friends and neighbors to ask them to quickly and quietly spread the word and to explain how they could flee south in the group's care or on their own. Or they could go into hiding with their help. Though a few refused to believe mass arrests could happen—especially to women and children—in most cases, everyone they communicated with chose to flee or hide. False papers had to be speedily arranged. A person named Night Watch was involved. He and his team of forgers apparently got no sleep for five days and five nights. Sometimes, because of illness or age or special health problems, some children or some adults were escorted without their family members. Those who needed special attention came as soon as possible *after* the others had left, as special needs required extra time. At the end of this paragraph, she writes, 'God help us if these families don't get reunited!'"

Sophie held up a finger for quiet as she reread one last passage. Everyone was silent. When she was done, she looked up and said, "Dahlia's account ends by talking about that policeman . . . Arnaud Boucher." She closed the book. "We need to call Chevy."

29

NEVER ASSUME

An hour later, the six of them stood in the bakery storage room amid boxes and flour bags and watched as Chevy crawled out of the chamber they'd discovered. He was followed after a moment by Boucher, who awkwardly half-crawled, half-rolled through the low opening, then stood up, dusted off his jacket, and took a quick swipe across his bald head.

"He looks anxious," Ben whispered to Jake.

"So the book was true. There *is* a cavern of possessions. Good. Many people will be happy," Boucher said softly.

"Happy? I thought you were trying to keep this information secret?" Claire said.

"Why would you think that?" Boucher replied.

"The guards—they brought you the book! We assumed you were trying to stop anyone from finding this place," Jake said.

"Ah, the guards. Well, they mistook my statement at the police station for support. But I was just upholding the law. This young lady was trespassing. When they arrived at my house with the book, I was surprised, of course, but I accepted the book and then sent them away. The next morning, I was on my way to bring it to our forensic documentation department for validation. But you took it from me," Boucher said with surprising composure.

Jake's throat dried instantly. *We assumed he was bad. What a mistake!*

"But now I see that the book *was* genuine. I suppose you brought me here to tell me what I already know—that my grandfather supported the Nazis," Boucher replied.

"No! Now it is you who have made an incorrect assumption. You don't know the whole story," Sophie said.

"What do you mean?" Boucher said, betraying irritation for the first time. But Sophie didn't quail.

"At first, your grandfather was helping Dahlia and the others in her network hide Jewish people's valuables. Then later, he assisted in transporting families to safety. He was a spy. He would tell Dahlia the plans of the Nazis and their collaborators—the French police—and would do everything to help *her* and defeat *them!*"

"But how is that possible? You know as well as I what the word *serpent* means!" Boucher said.

"Yes, I know. But that word has *another* meaning. It's all here—in this book. *Serpent* was the name of the secret operation to save Jewish treasures—and then Jewish lives!—that Dahlia's group organized. I've been thinking about this: she was a language teacher, so maybe she was recalling the word's Latin and Greek origins—it meant to *creep* or *crawl.* They had to stay out of sight, after all. Whatever that name meant, they succeeded because of their connections. And your grandfather, who was *not* a Nazi sympathizer, was *one* of those connections. He helped Dahlia from the beginning. She mentions gratitude to her dentist, Benjamin Spiegel, for making the introduction. She writes that your grandfather realized that if he could rise in the ranks of the police force, he could help Dahlia's group and others. He's the one who told Dahlia as soon as he found out about the roundup, the arrest of foreign-born Jews in Paris planned for July 1942. And he's the one who told her that the date had been moved because of Bastille Day—from July 13th through the 15th to the 16th through the 17th. He said that the French police were going to tell Jews that they were going to be taken away to work somewhere. But Dahlia knew that was a lie. She knew plenty of men who had been arrested, never to return. And your grandfather confirmed it. He told her to tell everyone that infants and old, infirm people were going to be taken away, too, so how could it be true that *work* was in their future? That's how Dahlia convinced so many people to flee. To further assist, she writes, your grandfather made sure that those few officers who were secretly sympathetic to the Resistance were the ones to check identification papers as people left Paris. Because of that, hundreds of people made it safely south to the Free Zone, where they were immediately placed in the hands of other groups, like the Eclaireurs Israélites de France and the Oeuvre de Secours aux Enfants—the Jewish Scouts of France and the Children's Aid Society. These groups took the youngsters traveling alone into their orphanages. Adults and families were driven by members of Dahlia's network to farms in rural areas, or to hotels or schools, or escorted to other safe places. Some went to mountain villages, such as Le Chambon-sur-Lignon, an entire town devoted to saving Jews and others facing persecution. Dahlia notes that it was lucky that Jews were not required to wear the yellow star in the Free Zone. Some went to the Italian Zone in southeastern France. Finally, those who could not or would not travel were hidden in Paris with French Christian families or Jews who were not foreign-born . . . hidden by your grandfather!"

"May I see that book?" Boucher extended a trembling hand for the volume.

Jake watched intently, as the policeman flipped through the last pages, his face softening. *He understands! He realizes it's all true.*

"My grandfather *wasn't* a traitor. He was a *hero*," Boucher whispered, wiping away a tear. "My father told me that near the end of my grandfather's life, he would tell stories from the war, stories that if true—and not just confused memories—implied that he was involved with the Nazis. Now I see that while he was seen to be working with them, he was actually a spy. *Mon dieu*." Boucher closed the book and looked around the cavern.

"What amazing people your great-grandmother and my grandfather were. To rescue all those people and to save all of this." Boucher motioned with his hand at the massive collection of items visible in the flickering light.

"Thank you for bringing me here. Thank you for being so persistent. I'm sorry I didn't support you back at the station." Boucher put his hand out to shake Sophie's, and she took it.

"*C'est d'accord*," she said with a smile.

"Well," Boucher added, clapping his hands together, "if there's anything *I* can ever do for *you*, I hope you won't hesitate to call on me."

"Hmm, there is *one* thing," Jake said, grinning.

30

FINALE!

The police cars, with sirens blaring and lights flashing, screeched to the curb in front of Le Cordon Bleu cooking school, where the final episode of the baking contest was about to begin filming live. Boucher flew out of the front seat and quickly opened the car's rear doors, allowing Ben, Heather, and Jake to clamber out.

The kids sprinted up the stairs, but Heather skidded to a stop right before the door.

"Dad?" she said.

Oliver Baker stood in the doorway with his hands on his hips and a stern look on his face.

Uh-oh, Jake thought.

Instinctively, both he and Ben reached for Heather's hands and clasped them in a sign of solidarity.

"Did you really think I wouldn't find out that my daughter was going to be on TV?" Mr. Baker asked.

"I'm sorry. I knew you wouldn't approve, but I needed to do this. I needed to see if I have what it takes," Heather replied. "Did you see the show, or did someone call you?"

"I found out the day after you applied. The TV director called to see if I would do an interview to help promote the show," he said.

Jake heard Heather swallow hard.

"So you've known about this the whole time?"

"I wanted to see if you'd go through with it. If you would have the gumption to disobey me and choose your own path. And you did. And . . . I'm proud." Mr. Baker's lips spread into a broad smile.

"I don't understand," Heather said.

"To be a world-class baker, you need drive. You need persistence and a sense of commitment. You've proved you have that." Mr. Baker bent down, reached into a bag at his feet, and pulled out a golden whisk. "Here, you might need this," he said, smiling.

"Oh, thank you!" Heather enveloped him in a big hug.

The show's director appeared, headset on and clipboard in her hand, and looked at the three muddy, limestone-dusted contestants in dismay. "Your clothes—" she began.

But before she could continue, Jenna appeared, breathless and holding a bag. "I'm glad you texted me. You three look, well . . . hopefully this all fits. It's the smallest size I had," she said to Heather, as she handed her a button-down blue cardigan and matching skirt. "Quick, go change!"

They looked considerably cleaner and neater when they emerged from the bathrooms a few minutes later, though Jake continued to brush limestone chips out of his hair. "There's still a lot of dust, I think. It's going to look terrible in high definition."

"Don't worry. You'll get used to appearing messy while cooking." Heather grinned at Jake and headed for her assigned station in front of Jake and Ben's.

"*Non*, there has been a change," the director said, as she motioned for Heather to join Ben at the boys' station. Jake, beaming, took Heather's solo spot.

"I don't understand," Heather said.

"Yeah, what's going on?" Ben asked the director.

But she just gestured at Jake, as if the explanation was up to him.

"I found a loophole in the rules," he said. "We can switch teammates. Or in this case, I can go alone while you two team together for the finale."

Ben grinned and turned to Heather and said, "Partners?"

"Definitely." She clasped her hand in his and turned to look at Jacques.

"Okay, contestants, you have three hours to bake a chocolate dessert. We want presentation and flavor to match, something fit for royalty. In other words—"

Here it comes, Jake thought.

"This should be your *crowning* achievement!" Jacques said as he started the clock.

Jake thought, *We've been up for more than 24 hours and found a huge collection of hidden heirlooms. How is it we're all still standing upright?* But as he pictured the reunion of families separated for decades, all thanks to the red leather-bound book they had found, he felt a burst of new energy. He glanced at Sophie, Claire, and Felix, who were watching from the wings and gave them a wink. *Now, where's the flour?*

Jake whipped up his batter and poured it into the Chicago Willis Tower–shaped baking tin that he and Ben had brought in case contestants were asked to bake something from their home countries. After getting his cake into the oven, he sat down and drew little sketches of people and dogs to adorn the top of the cake.

"Very nice," Ben said, glancing over at the figures Jake had drawn.

"Compliments of my right brain!" Jake grinned. He filled a pastry bag with melted caramel and slowly began to trace his pencil drawings. *Perfect. Once they cool, they will stand up nicely on the cake.*

Jake, Ben, Heather, and the Dutch team stood behind the presentation table. The Dutch team had gone for a *kransekake*, a traditional Scandinavian wreath cake. It had multiple tiers and was adorned with colorful characters making up a Norman Rockwell–like scene. It dominated the room.

Ben and Heather's four-tier cake had alternating dark and white chocolate frosting and a caramelized cherry sauce that tumbled down its tiers like a fruit river.

Jake watched as François and Meredith entered the room. He saw their eyes go immediately to the *kransekake*. They smiled but grinned even more broadly when they saw Heather and Ben's masterpiece. François frowned when he looked at Jake's cake, and Jake's heart sank a little. He thought it looked really good, though he knew it wasn't anything compared to the other teams' showstoppers.

"It appears that someone didn't take the word 'presentation' to heart," François said.

Just wait till you taste it, though, Jake thought.

"Oh, I don't know about that. The figurines are perfectly sized and shaped," Meredith said. Ben coughed to let Jake know he'd heard the compliment to Jake's artistic skills.

The judges moved to the Dutch team first and cut into the *kransekake*, pushing little pieces around on their plates.

"Good flavor, great presentation, but I'm afraid the texture isn't quite right," Meredith said.

Next they came to Ben and Heather's cake. "Impressive and creative," François said.

"The power of teamwork," Heather said as she clutched Ben's hand.

"*Oui.* Indeed," François said. "Bright cherry, but not so sharp as to drown out the white chocolate, which is quite hard to do. Well done," he nodded.

Jake's heart leapt for his friend's success. *A head nod!*

"And what is this?" François said.

"I call it 'Chicago's Stanley House Special,'" Jake said with a smile. "Inside joke. But since we're in France, I'm renaming it *Tour de Chocolat.*"

Meredith tasted it first. "This is amazing. It's simple, but the flavor is incredible. I think I'll have another bite." She winked at Jake as she dug her fork greedily into the slab of thickly frosted cake.

While François was not effusive in any way while sampling his piece, Jake thought he detected a *hint* of a grin.

*   *   *

As expected, Ben and Heather won the baking contest, with the Dutch team coming in second. Jake's chocolate cake received an honorable mention and proved a favorite with the film crew, who rapidly devoured it once the cameras were turned off.

31

HONOR AND REMEMBRANCE

Palais de l'Élysée
The Official Residence of the President of France

Within hours of finding the red notebook, Chevy had located Naomi, who was alive and well, living in Barcelona, Spain, where she had grown up. She knew that she had once lived in Paris and remembered having sisters, but she had no memory of names and so had never searched for them.

Now the two sisters, arm in arm, walked into the residence of the president of France.

Following Esther and Naomi were the six friends responsible for reuniting them. They took their seats in the Hall of Festivities—La Salle des Fêtes, the ballroom where presidents were inaugurated. Jake's head spun in every direction. The majestic chandeliers and red-draped windows, the gold-trimmed walls and splendid murals—all combined to create an air of opulence and graciousness.

The event had been organized quickly to allow everyone to attend, since Jake, Ben, Heather, and Felix would be leaving Paris soon. But there was no sign of haste or cut corners. To begin the program, select players from the French National

Orchestra played "La Marseillaise," the country's national anthem. As they stood, Jake hummed along and squeezed Sophie's hand, nodding toward Esther and Naomi. Esther was standing on the other side of Sophie and had a firm grip around her sister's shoulder.

"I just saw on my tablet that Felix's story about the cavern was picked up by the Associated Press. Before the day is over, I bet it will be in at least 50 newspapers around the world," Ben whispered.

"Sweet. He'll have no problem getting a scholarship now," Jake responded.

A hush fell over the crowd as the president entered and made her way to the podium. She looked toward the audience with a warm smile on her face. "Ladies and gentlemen, honored guests, *bienvenue*—welcome. The Ordre National de la Légion d'honneur is our highest military and civilian award. This order of merit was established by Napoleon Bonaparte on May 19, 1802. I am confident that even he could never have imagined our reason for celebrating today, as our gathering together juxtaposes life's darkest hour with its brightest moments: cruelty and courage . . . savagery and sacrifice. It is my privilege at this time, as grand master of the order, to posthumously bestow this medal to Arnaud Boucher, who showed exceptional heroism during a time of war, risking his life while using his position in our city's Police Nationale to aid in the escape of countless persecuted Jews in Paris."

On cue, newly promoted Capitaine Boucher walked down the aisle to accept the medal for his grandfather.

"Arnaud Boucher is going to go down in history in France," Jake said.

"Yes, and who knows," Sophie whispered, "maybe he'll be named a Righteous Gentile by the World Holocaust Remembrance Center in Jerusalem. Think of it, Jake: Yad Vashem!"

Arnaud Boucher's proud grandson vowed, as he accepted the medal from the president, to live up to his grandfather's courage and integrity for the rest of his days.

"Before I invite our next two guests to join me," the president continued, "I am pleased to announce that I have formed a special task force that will work tirelessly to make sure that families listed in the now-famous red and blue journals will be—if they have been separated—united. There is no more important task before us as a nation than bringing family members together. This group will connect relatives, many of whom may not know their own family stories, as well as return their long-lost possessions. To oversee these vital operations, Commandant Bellamy Chevrolet will report directly to me to ensure swift and expeditious reunions." With that announcement, she clapped and nodded her head toward a beaming Chevy. Jake swiveled in his chair, grinning, and clasped his hand firmly in his friend's. Chevy, resplendent in his dress uniform, winked and smiled back.

A moment later, the audience gasped as two tall, impeccably dressed soldiers marched down the aisle and stopped directly in front of Esther and Naomi. With military precision, they bent down and offered their arms for support.

Jake felt a tingle shoot up his spine as he watched the soldiers escort his great-aunts onto the stage.

The president embraced them both and took their hands. "As a mother, I cannot imagine the courage that your mother, Dahlia Schneyer, found to send her children away to safety so that she could continue to save others' lives. She is a credit to her adopted homeland, France. We are indebted to her for her example of heroism and for the ideals she upheld as she fought against man's inhumanity to man. We now know that approximately 13,000 foreign-born and stateless Jews throughout Paris were rounded up by about 9,000 French civil servants—almost half of whom were police—and then killed at Auschwitz. The number of victims would have been greater, though, but for the efforts of Arnaud Boucher and your mother, along with members of her rescue team and the others throughout Paris who, under Dahlia's leadership, swiftly jumped into action to warn, to assist, to save lives. And when Dahlia's group connected with those other individuals and groups along the border of the Free Zone, the destiny of those Jews was rewritten."

The president opened a box to reveal the red-ribboned medal. "It is my honor to posthumously award Dahlia Schneyer the Ordre National de la Légion d'honneur. We are also pleased to announce that a monument to her will be erected and placed at the entrance to the grotto of the Parc des Buttes Chaumont. While we do not know how she died, in a way, that is a blessing, for we won't have to dwell on her last moments at the hands of the Nazis. Instead, we will celebrate her life as a wife and a mother—as a woman of valor—who answered the call of her people in need with a devotion and selflessness that we can all aspire to. When the monument is ready, we hope that you will join us for the unveiling ceremony. I look forward to retracing her steps over the suspension bridge as we help our citizens and visitors in the years to come learn her story . . . and never forget."

All of the guests rose to their feet and applauded enthusiastically as Esther and Naomi held the open box together.

* * *

After a slew of official press photos, the invited guests—representatives of the police force and prominent members of the Jewish community—all said their goodbyes and departed. The president herself stayed long enough for Jake to have a photograph taken with her, a memento he knew he would always cherish.

"Come here, kids." It was Chevy's voice, deep but soft. Jake, Ben, Sophie, Heather, Claire, and Felix all gathered around him.

"You look pretty sharp, Chevy," Heather said.

"Yeah, and a double promo past *capitaine* all the way to *commandant*. That's impressive," Jake commented. "And well deserved."

"Thanks to all of you," Chevy smiled. "Listen, while I know we will see each other soon—at least I hope so—I wanted to take this opportunity to express my gratitude. It has been an incredible experience getting to know you and to be a part of your journey here. I don't think this city will ever be quite the same for me again. And you'd better keep in touch. If you don't, I will use my new rank to put you all on the world's most-wanted list." Chevy's grin lit up the room. Not even the two-ton chandelier suspended above them could compete with it.

The six of them swarmed Chevy and enveloped him in a hug. As they gripped each other tightly, Sophie spoke. "We will be close forever—I know it. We met because of history, and together we faced our fears, came to each other's rescue, and supported each other with a camaraderie I've never known before. We solved an impossible riddle, and in the process, reunited my Bubbe's family—one of many family reunions to come."

But it was Jake who had the last word. "Yes, we will be close . . . and we will *always* remember Paris."

32
À BIENTÔT

"Bubbe, you didn't need to come all the way to the airport to see us off," Jake said as he hugged her.

"Every minute I have left will be with family. Even if it means a taxi ride." Esther's smile spread ear to ear. "Besides, I have to give you a few things. But you can't open them until you are halfway home."

Sophie handed Ben a large box tied with string, and Jake a small one covered in colorful wrapping paper.

"This is rugelach," Ben said, inhaling the aroma. "I could smell it from a hundred feet away."

"Well, there's one surprise gone. Now seriously though, don't open the other box until you are over the Atlantic," Sophie said as she hugged Jake.

"You'll come to New York this summer, right?" Jake asked Sophie.

"Yes, I can't wait for you to show me American architecture," she replied. "But you should keep August free. Bubbe and I are trying to organize a big reunion of all of Naomi's family. Bubbe hasn't been to Barcelona, so we will take a train there. Naomi has four children, 12 grandchildren, and 15 great-grandchildren."

"Wouldn't miss it," Jake said.

"You'd better come, too, Ben. You are family just as much as Jake." Sophie hugged Ben.

"Thank you! I'll be the good-looking brother Jake never had." Ben playfully punched Jake in the arm.

The boys gave Esther and Sophie another hug and then reluctantly joined the security line to enter the airport.

*   *   *

"Jake, we're halfway," Ben said, as he took off his headphones.

Jake woke with a start. "Halfway? Oh, yeah . . . the small package. Now, where is it?" Jake dug around in his trusty backpack, still encrusted with mud.

"Did I tell you I found out that Claire is actually an accomplished ballerina?" Ben asked.

"You're kidding!" Jake replied.

"Nope. Once I knew her last name, I found an article on the internet about a teen ballet troupe. She was their lead last summer," Ben said.

"Incredible! I had a feeling she was hiding something important. Oh, here it is!" Jake pulled the present from his backpack, untied the bow, and tore the paper, revealing a felt-trimmed box with a clasp and a hinge. He undid the clasp and cracked open the box.

Ben gulped and Jake widened his eyes. The box held Dahlia's Ordre national de la Légion d'honneur.

Jake stared at the medal. "I don't believe it," he said.

"Wow. Looks like there's a note, Jake." Ben pulled out a piece of paper folded into the cover of the box and handed it to him.

Dear Jake,

I can think of no one better to safeguard this medal. Your courage, creativity, and tenacity are just like my mother's—your great-grandmother Dahlia's. I know she would be as proud of you as I am.

All my love,
Bubbe

"Whoa." Jake breathed heavily as he gently touched the medal.

"I agree with Bubbe," Ben said, peering over his best friend's shoulder.

*   *   *

After the flight attendant removed their dinner trays, Jake asked, "What's next, Ben? How do we top this?" Jake tapped the box with the medal inside.

"Who says we have to top it? I mean, adventures are like roller coasters. Just because we rode the tallest one doesn't mean the others aren't fun," Ben said.

"You should start baking fortune cookies so you can put those little gems in them." Jake grinned.

"I'll drink to that. *L'chaim*, Jake." Ben raised his glass of soda to his best friend.

"*L'chaim*, Ben." Jake smiled and raised his glass in return.

"You know, you're two years overdue for your bar mitzvah," Ben said.

"You're joking, right?" Jake replied.

"No, you could have the ceremony at the Western Wall in Jerusalem. Come on, Jake. A trip to Israel! I'll teach you how to speak and read Hebrew. We're bound to have some great times there. And the architecture—you'll love it!"

Jake laughed.

"And did I ever tell you about the stars at Masada? You haven't lived until you've seen the night sky at the base of that mountain. It's fantastic!"

"Sounds amazing . . . And one thing is true: No matter where we go, as long as we're together, somehow I know it will be—"

"Epic!" they said in unison.

ACKNOWLEDGEMENTS AND AUTHOR'S NOTE

ACKNOWLEDGEMENTS

For their careful attention to details and historical facts and their enthusiasm for this story, I would like to express my deepest gratitude to my publisher; to my editors, Emma Walton Hamilton and Anne Himmelfarb; to Paul Frieden, a retired labor lawyer and a valued reader; and to historian Avinoam Patt, Ph.D., the Doris and Simon Konover Chair of Judaic Studies and the Director of the Center for Judaic Studies and Contemporary Jewish Life at the University of Connecticut.

AUTHOR'S NOTE

While *Paris Secrets* does not go into many details about the Holocaust—the murder of six million European Jews by Nazi Germany and its collaborators between 1933 and 1945—it is the backdrop for the novel, which is a modern-day story of adventure, courage, and discovering one's roots.

It is difficult to read about the Holocaust, but it is, nevertheless, vital for everyone to understand what can happen when we let fear, dislike, or hatred of other people guide our actions and decisions. The type of bias or prejudice that led to the Holocaust is not a thing of the past. I urge everyone to learn about different cultures and resist assigning labels to entire groups of people. People should be judged as individuals, by their words and actions, not by their membership in some group.

Separating Fact From Fiction

Paris Secrets is a work of fiction, but I was inspired by real people and places and historic events to write my novel.

People: The character of Dahlia Schneyer was inspired by several Jewish heroines in France during World War II.
Read more here:
https://jwa.org/encyclopedia/article/
resistance-jewish-organizations-in-france-1940-1944

Rose Valland (1898-1980) was a real person—a teacher, art historian, and French heroine of the Resistance.
Learn more here:
https://www.monumentsmenfoundation.org/
valland-capt-rose
The forger, Night Watch, was based on actual forgers, such as Adolfo Kaminsky and Oscar Rosowsky.

You may be wondering how Esther's two younger sisters made it safely to Spain and Switzerland. It was made possible by two humanitarian undertakings. Even though these missions could not be explained in the story (because Esther/Bubbe was unaware of their existence), it is exciting to share this information with you now.

The heroic Spanish rescuer was Eduardo Propper de Callejón, the "wartime Spanish first secretary in Bordeaux."

Learn his story here:

https://www.yadvashem.org/righteous/stories/propper-de-callejon.html

https://www.dailymail.co.uk/femail/article-7734811/My-Grandparents-War-viewers-left-tears-Helena-Bonham-Carter-discovers-war-hero-grandfather.html

Swiss charities: "From 1940, Swiss charities provided large-scale humanitarian aid to war-stricken children, offering short-stay evacuations of over 60,000 French, Belgian and Yugoslav children to Swiss families, including at least some French Jewish children. In summer 1942, however, when French authorities began the round-ups of Jews, this approach faltered."

Learn more here:

https://www.euppublishing.com/doi/full/10.3366/nfs.2020.0283

Places: The Parc des Buttes Chaumont in Paris—with its grassy fields, beautiful lake, island, temple, bridges, and grotto with waterfall—exists and is a hidden gem in France's capital city. However, the passageway under the lake is fictional.

The Opéra national de Paris—with its underground lake and rich history—and the Catacombs are also real.

Read more about these places:

https://en.parisinfo.com/paris-museum-monument/71468/Parc-des-Buttes-Chaumont

https://www.parisinsidersguide.com/parc-des-buttes-chaumont.html

https://www.operadeparis.fr/en

https://www.operadeparis.fr/en/visits/palais-garnier

https://www.catacombes.paris.fr/en

Things: I've included some little-known but true stories. People hid valuables in jars filled with goo, and placed forged IDs in sandwiches loaded with mayonnaise, knowing that the Nazis would not look too closely in order to keep their uniforms clean. These facts were merged in chapter 28.

Read more about it: Marcel Marceau, rescuer, and mayonnaise:

https://medium.com/lessons-from-history/french-mime-artist-who-saved-children-in-world-war-ii-marcel-marceau-fac01f711dfa

Events: It is important to know that there was an actual roundup of approximately 13,000 foreign-born Jews, of whom at least 4,000 were children (including French Jewish children of foreign-born parents), in Paris on July 16–17, 1942. When Nazi Germany first occupied France, the Jewish population was approximately 320,000. Of these, approximately 75,000 (more than 50,000 Parisian Jews, including those thousands arrested in the July 1942 roundup) were deported to Nazi death camps, where almost all perished.

Dahlia's Operation Serpent is the name of a fictional mission to save Jewish possessions and, ultimately, Jewish lives over the course of just a few days in the summer of 1942 before what became known as the Vel' d'Hiv' roundup. Sadly, Dahlia's mission did not actually happen. This novel presents a what-if scenario and demonstrates how a relatively small number of people can make a tremendous difference to humanity. Even one person can.

Just as Dahlia was based on real-life French Jewish heroines, the fictional character Arnoud Boucher has a real-life counterpart in a man named Charles Létoffé, "a police officer responsible for foreign citizens in wartime France . . . post-humously honoured as a Righteous Among the Nations by

Yad Vashem for his role in saving Jews during the Holocaust. Charles Létoffé lived with his family in Soissons, north of Paris, where he was able to utilise his role to both hide Jews [in his own home] from the Nazis and to warn them of impending round-ups. The honour was presented to his son Bernard Létoffé by Daniel Saada of the Israeli embassy in Paris . . ."

Read more here:
December 2017: https://eurojewcong.org/news/communities-news/france/french-policeman-posthumously-honoured-righteous-nations/#:~:text=A%20police%20officer%20responsible%20for%20foreign%20citizens%20in,his%20role%20in%20saving%20Jews%20during%20the%20Holocaust

Jewish Lifesaving Groups in France: Eclaireurs Israélites de France—the Jewish Scouts of France—was one of several organizations, including the Oeuvre de Secours aux Enfants (the Children's Aid Society) and the Mouvement des Jeunesses Sionistes (the Zionist Youth Movement) that rescued between 12,000 and 15,000 Jewish children in France.

Such humanitarian work took place across Europe over the course of the war.

Other groups: You may be familiar with the story of Nicholas Winton and his rescue of at least 669 Jewish children, who from 1938 to 1939 were taken from Czechoslovakia to Great Britain through a mission called the Kindertransport.

There was even an entire village in France dedicated to saving lives:
https://encyclopedia.ushmm.org/content/en/article/le-chambon-sur-lignon

* * *

In the late 18th century, 90 percent of the world's Jewish population lived in Europe. In 1933, about 60 percent of the world's Jewish population—9.5 million Jews of the 15.3 million worldwide—lived in Europe. By 1950, five years after the Holocaust, only 3.5 million Jews remained in Europe. And today, about 1.3 million Jews live in Europe, two-thirds of whom are in the UK, Germany, and France.

*   *   *

While Jake, Ben, Sophie, Bubbe, Heather, Claire, Felix, and Chevy sprang from my imagination, I hope the depiction of their friendship—and their discoveries about a person's capacity to act bravely in the face of inhumanity—will serve to inspire you to keep in your mind—and etched on your heart—this one undeniable truth:

Another person's pain ends where your act of kindness, courage, or compassion begins.

There is a saying from the Talmud: "A person who saves one life saves the world entire." When I think of those words, I cannot help but see how every person represents an entire world to a mother, a father, a sister, a brother, a grandparent, an aunt, an uncle, or a friend. If we can just keep the preciousness of each person in mind as we go through life, then we will all be doing our part to save the world.

— Sean Vogel

Made in the USA
Middletown, DE
01 July 2021